How to Paint
MURALS &
TROMPE
L'OEIL

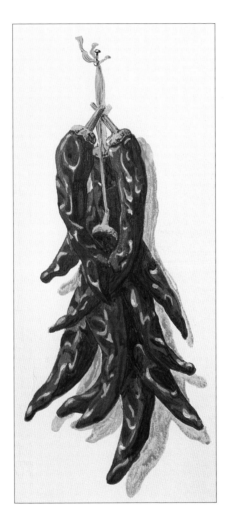

How to Paint
MURALS &
TROMPE
L'OEIL

VICTORIA ELLERTON
with SIMON BRADY

C&B
COLLINS & BROWN

For my parents,
Patrick and Alison
Victoria Ellerton

To Laura, Daniel and Adam,
with love
Simon Brady

First published in Great Britain in 2000
by Collins & Brown Limited, London House,
Great Eastern Wharf, Parkgate Road
London SW11 4NQ

Copyright ©
Collins & Brown
Limited 2000

Text copyright ©
Victoria Ellerton
with Simon Brady 2000

Photographs copyright ©
see copyright holders on page 128

The right of Victoria Ellerton and
Simon Brady to be identified
as the authors of this work has
been asserted by them in accordance
with the Copyright, Designs and
Patents Act, 1988.

9 8 7 6 5 4 3 2 1

British Library Cataloguing-in-Publication Data: A
catalogue record for this book is available from
the British Library.

ISBN 1 85585 7596

Project managed and edited by
Jane Donovan
Art direction and design by
Jane Forster
Special photography by Edward
Allwright, assisted by Alex Giordano
and Ian Whitbread
Styling by Jane Forster
Template illustrations by Terry Evans
Reproduction by Hong Kong
Graphic and Printing Ltd
Printed and bound at Sing
Cheong Printing Co. Ltd,
Hong Kong

Contents

Foreword

Knocking down barriers has always appealed to me. On this occasion, it is the awesome thought of the large blank wall, oozing with intimidation, looming and waiting for its colour and design. This is the daunting barrier I hope to chip away and finally flatten for you.

The game of painting, like so many, is about confidence. I hope to bathe you in it, to show you the way and to underline how mistakes don't matter but can be learnt from and rectified. With essential guidelines, a range of projects waits to be achieved. A little familiarity with holding a brush is your only requirement. Swathes of mystique and pretension can often cloud the subject and remove the fun. Our examples aim to cut these out, to be direct and uncluttered, and aspire to restoring that fun. Like overcooked vegetables, sloppily painted murals and trompe l'oeil are to be avoided at all times. Our aim is to encourage the 'al dente' crunch which leads to slick wall decorations of which you will not tire. Technique is just as important as artistry.

Enjoy following our demonstrated projects and hey presto, before you know it, you will have taken a leap into the unknown and created that mural, painted floor or trompe l'oeil that you've always wondered whether or not you could do.

Victoria Ellerton.

Paradoxically, the highest compliment you can receive as a trompe l'oeil artist is silence. It was the ultimate accolade when my son's friend tried to switch on the light using my painted light switch. I have always been fascinated by the skills of the artist who can transform pencil lines and paint into a perfect representation of three-dimensional objects. Whether the subject is a solid piece of wood or a delicate Venetian wine glass, the illusion is achieved by careful observation and equally careful application of paint. I hope that this book will show you some of the tricks and uncover some of the daunting mysteries that can seem so intimidating when you start.

I cannot stress enough how important it is to look at the object you are trying to depict. Don't paint a brass key, paint the brass key in front of you. There is no substitute for practice and nothing more satisfying than when you achieve what you have aimed for. But the real point is to enjoy the process and to have fun. I have had a great time doing the book and I hope that you enjoy it as much. Thanks to Vicky for including me on this project and for keeping a straight face when it really mattered.

Introduction

From Egyptian tombs to Las Vegas hotel rooms, the need to create designs on walls has always been an enduring and natural instinct. This book is designed for those people who harbour a wish to paint a mural or trompe l'oeil, but lack the courage to try.

Scant use of perspective and minimal measuring contribute to an easy ride for the beginner. Each project is broken down into step-by-step photographs with explanatory captions. The simplest of projects, such as Outside-in and the Red hot chilli peppers (pages 42–3 and 60–1) are

Horizon lines are restful. Despite the strong colours used in this mural, the overall impression is one of calm. The scene is uncluttered and simple with the vivid shapes and contrasting bright colours adding a quiet clarity. Here, the majority of the mural is achieved with blocked-in colour and the post, rope and seagull's wing are the only detailed areas.

Painted in 1395 in the bridal chamber of the Florentine Palazzo Davanzati, this mural (left) depicts a legend and commemorates an illustrious marriage of the time. The figures and stylized trees are framed with decorative columns and rows of panels beneath.

Look through the trellised arch (right) and you will be led up a flagstone path to the central stone fountain and hedge beyond. A fine three-dimensional quality is to be found in this classic composition.

achieved in a mere four steps. It should be noted that once the designs were conceived on paper and the wall prepared, none of them took more than a day to execute. A keen beginner, with a little enthusiasm and application, should crack a project in under a week.

The murals and floors supply decorative backdrops rather than painstaking works of art and the trompe l'oeil section explains simply the rudiments of this specialized art. There is a variety of subject matter, scale and style, with strong use of colour and a feeling for space. The first part of the book is devoted to the seven mural and three painted floor projects. These are largely graphic in style, with techniques such as 'blocking in' and 'cutting in' used throughout. This is followed by the eight trompe l'oeil projects. These guide you through the tricks of the highlight and shadow, and

remind you of the importance of taking a long, hard look at your subject. Trompe l'oeil is a French expression meaning 'to fool the eye'. It is a game played between the artist and the spectator, who enjoys being deceived and uncovering the trick.

The project template section (pages 114–121) gives examples of stencils used. These shapes and sizes may be enlarged or reduced from the book and used for your own design. The paint directory (pages 108–113) provides a precise reminder of every colour that is used or mixed in the demonstrations. In the basics section (pages 72–85), the brushes, tools and types of paint needed are described and you will find further information on several paint finishes and other helpful tips, such as how to transfer your design to the wall; also a basic list of essential equipment. Finally, photographs of artists' work are reproduced in Inspirations (pages 86–107) to encourage you and to show you the true potential of your newly acquired skills.

MURALS AND FLOORS

Brilliant brush strokes

The painting of walls is the most important, widely used and the earliest of all forms of wall decoration. Egypt is the chief storehouse for some of the most ancient examples. These include sacred symbols such as the vulture, painted on ceilings, and horizontal bands of figures on the walls. In the following demonstrated mural and floor projects,

there is repeated use of time-saving devices such as pre-cut stencils and low-tack masking tape to achieve shapes and straight lines fast and effectively. With the exception of Up, up and away (see pages 14–17), Cave creation (see pages 20–3) and the Mock stone floor (see pages 30–1), all the projects are painted with pure and simple blocked-in colour. This is a technique that requires application, rather than artistic skill. Carefully explained examples of paint finishes appear in several of the projects and acrylic glaze forms the basis of all the techniques used.

As an alternative to carpet and other surfaces, a painted floor is

This graphic mural, inspired by Patrick Caulfield, (left) proves how the simple things in life are often the easiest and can be the best. Straight-forward lines with three images within the window is all it takes. It is precision, rather than artistic ability that is required here.

Like the window (above), the kilim-inspired painted floor (below) is reliant on neatness and accuracy. Tram lines of low-tack masking tape are used to achieve the straight painted edges and lines, while geometric stencils spirit the motifs into place.

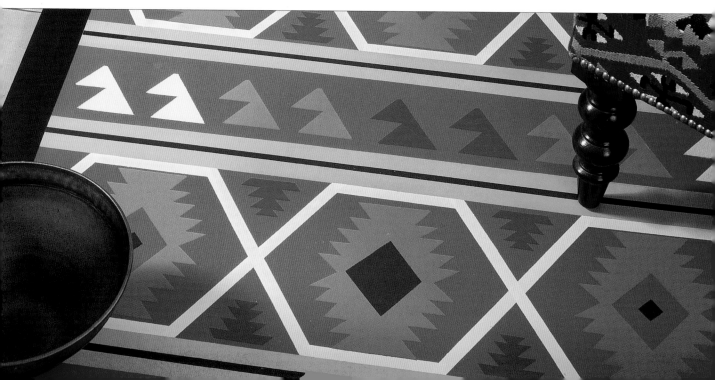

often a refreshing decorative solution. The three examples boast a purposeful sense of design but are distinctly different in character. The Mock stone floor and Flower-strewn floor (see below and pages 30–1 and 36–7) are painted with an airy spacious area in mind, while the vibrant kilim design (see below and pages 26–9) could happily sit in a wintry room beside a blazing fire.

If you are painting on existing wooden floors, be sure they are stripped of all varnish before you begin. If they are not, the paint will refuse to adhere properly and will flake off easily. Once the painted floors are completely dry, it is vital to varnish them with several coats of tough acrylic floor varnish.

The varnishing of murals is only necessary if they may be fingered by children or are to be situated in a kitchen or bathroom where heat and steam prevail. Many of the mural and floor projects lend themselves to certain areas of the home and suggestions are given with the instructions. Some projects have been designed with children in mind, but every scheme is versatile. Your own individual taste dictates the style to which you are drawn and its destined position within your home.

The classic design of this stone and granite painted floor (right) ensures it will always be easy to live with. Once the measuring and drawing of the lines has been done, the hard work is over. The frottage paint finish (page 82) used to produce the stone slabs is one of the most creative and satisfying of all techniques. Sponging is used to achieve the simple granite effect.

Great fun is waiting to be had when you paint these bison on their textured background (above). The strong emphasis on loose paint finishes, such as frottage and sponging, means you can let your hair down, forget about precision and be free with your tinted layers of acrylic glaze.

Up, up and away

This floating apparition is a joyful sight for a child's eyes. Indeed, the thought of flying in one's own balloon amongst the clouds as the ground rushes past below is an exciting prospect for anyone. Ideal for children's bedrooms and playrooms, this mural would also work well if it was painted up a staircase.

Stylized and old-fashioned in character, this onion shaped hot-air balloon defies the twenty-first century. The intrepid travellers, complete with telescope and red handkerchief, exude a simple charm. A perpendicular anchor and sandbags underline the jaunty angle of the balloon and basket to emphasize the balloon being blown along by gusts of wind in a gentle, cloudy blue sky.

COLOUR PALETTE
You will need white plus the colours below (see Paint Directory, pages 108–113).

Planning the design

A painted background of sky blue vinyl silk emulsion (latex) was softened with white glaze and the image of the balloon and figures was then transferred to the wall using the tracing method (see page 77). The angle of the balloon was experimented with initially by holding the tracing against the wall at different angles.

1 Mix a white acrylic glaze (see page 76) and apply it with a household brush to the sky blue background. To produce more density, give clouded areas a heavier amount of glaze. Work the clouds in areas of about 1 sq m (10½ sq ft), then complete steps 2 and 3 and finally, apply another section of glaze until the wall of sky is complete.

2 Bunch a muslin rag in your hand and gently rag the glaze in a loose, circular motion until the original brush strokes have completely disappeared.

3 Here, the badger softener is used to miraculously soften and unite the glaze (see page 75).

Tilting the basket slightly gave the impression that the top-hatted gentleman was able to focus on his subject more easily. You will find that painting the balloon at an angle gives life and movement to the mural.

Blocking in the balloon with colour was a simple process: a steady hand and compliant brush are needed to achieve a nice crisp edge. Stripes and swags were traced into position and blocked in. The stencil used to create texture on the basket (see page 78) saved time and low-tack masking tape was used as a guide to accuracy when painting the anchor and ropes.

YOU WILL NEED

Household brushes for preparation of wall
Badger softener
Medium-sized and large fitches
Fine and medium-sized artist's brushes
Tracing paper
Cutting mat
Stencil card
Scalpel
Basic equipment (see page 74)

4 The previously-traced images of the balloon, basket and figures are then blocked in in the appropriate colours (see page 79). Here, the last patch of balloon is blocked in with a large fitch.

5 When the paint is dry, trace stripes onto the onion shaped balloon and then apply the darker yellow colour using a medium-sized fitch.

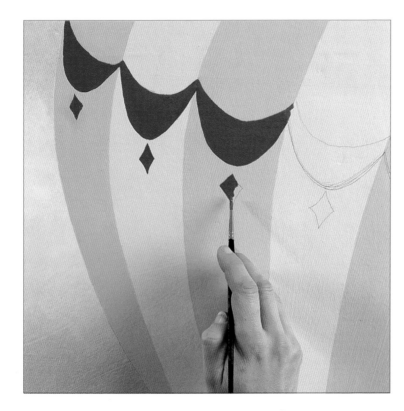

6 Next, trace the decorative swags and diamonds in position and apply the red paint with a medium-sized artist's brush.

7 To create the texture on the basket, cut a stencil (see page 78), position it with low-tack masking tape and use a fitch to stipple in soft raw umber.

8 Give some definition to the base of the basket using the same colour as step 7 and a fine artist's brush.

9 Now carefully paint in the previously drawn sandbags using a dark bluish purple and an artist's brush.

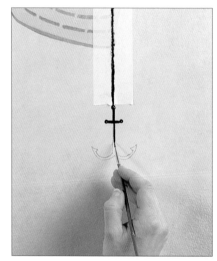

10 Once again, use an artist's brush to carefully paint in the already-drawn, delicate shape of the telescope with the same shade of purple as the sandbags.

11 Apply low-tack masking tape either side of the ruled line for the anchor rope and then paint in the rope and complete the previously-drawn hanging anchor in black. Remove the masking tape.

DEPICTING SKIES

Skies hold universal appeal and they are a popular backdrop for many murals. The sky that surrounds the hot-air balloon is soft and powdery, the clouds being of cumulus formation. While stratus clouds are elongated horizontals and cirrus clouds feather-like sprawls, it is the cumulus cloud that is easiest for the beginner to experiment with.

Painting a sky can unleash hidden moods and be highly therapeutic. No two individuals' skies will ever be the same. Like handwriting, it will brandish your character and convey your temperament.

A haunting sunset demands confident brushwork and use of colour. Several layers of acrylic glazes are necessary to achieve the right colour density, while the technique of laying on the glaze, ragging and softening remains the same.

12 Draw the balloon ropes in with a pencil and ruler first. Apply low-tack masking tape as in step 11 and then use a fitch to paint in the rope lines in a soft grey. Remove the masking tape.

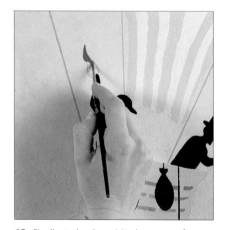

13 Finally, to lend a spirited gesture of farewell, fill in the already-drawn handkerchief in the same red as the swags and diamonds on the balloon.

Nocturnal city skyline

Absorbed into the background of conversation and culinary activity, this mural is a glamorous panorama. The twinkling skyline of Rome at night is both powerfully strong and delicately soft. A dark background, lit by the gold moon, stars and pale yellow windows, results in a glittering apparition. It is tailor-made for romantic celebrations and fantastically quick and easy to execute.

YOU WILL NEED
Household brushes for preparation of wall
Rome travel book
Charcoal
Fine and medium-sized artist's brushes
Tracing paper
Cutting mat
Stencil card
Scalpel
Large fitch
Adhesive spray
Basic equipment (see page 74)

COLOUR PALETTE
You will need the colours below (see Paint Directory, pages 108–113).

Your key to success is an illustrative book of Rome. Choose your favourite architectural shapes and compress their silhouettes in a skyline drawing on paper. Remember: you are aiming for the flavour of the capital, not a photographic reproduction, so don't worry about correct locations of buildings. First, block in the upper section of the wall in a deep blue matt emulsion (latex), then copy your drawing in larger scale onto the wall at eye-level. Use charcoal for this as it will show up better against the dark background.

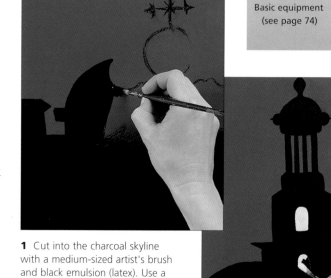

1 Cut into the charcoal skyline with a medium-sized artist's brush and black emulsion (latex). Use a finer brush for the more awkward edges. Complete all the black blocking in down to skirting (baseboard) level. First draw, then paint a few single-arched windows in freehand with pale yellow.

2 To save time, stencils were cut for the rows of smaller windows. Here, a set of three arched windows is held in position with low-tack masking tape and stippled with a fitch and pale yellow.

3 Now draw in the moon, then paint it with gold metallic paint. One layer only will create an interesting shaded depth.

4 Star stencils were also cut in advance and stuck to the wall with adhesive spray. Here, they are stippled with gold metallic paint. Beware of a tendency to fill the sky with stars. Restrain yourself: less is certainly more in this case.

Cave creation

COLOUR PALETTE
You will need the colours below (see Paint Directory, pages 108–113).

If the stresses of the twenty-first century are getting to you, why not retreat to the simplicity of the cave? Here, the earth colours and their textured treatment for the cave wall are both comforting and restful; the primitive bison are candid, with the obvious hand print and suggestion of cracks producing cavernous impressions. The layers of tinted acrylic glaze that build up the textured finish are fun to do and there is lots of room for experiment in this particular project. Areas that may appear to be 'a mistake' at first, can be softened and worked over later. Everything can be rectified!

Planning the design

A naive painting such as this creates an entirely different atmosphere. It is the type of mural that could be successfully painted on every wall in the room. Large areas may be left in the plainer earth colours, giving more of a paint finished texture, while the bison shapes are left to frolic on only a couple of walls. The overall effect is warm and all-encompassing, and is recommended for small bedrooms in cool climates, rather than large ones in sticky cities. Follow the steps below and once you have prepared the walls with an off-white vinyl silk emulsion (latex), be free with your brush strokes and make the most of that final hand print to sign off your creative wall.

1 Mix up a yellow ochre acrylic glaze (see page 76) and apply it to the wall in sections of about 1sq m (10½sq ft) at a time. Frottage each section quickly as you go along (see page 82) with a sheet of newspaper.

2 Once the first layer of frottaged glaze is dry, mix up a thin burnt sienna acrylic glaze. Apply this in similar sized sections and gently sponge (see page 80). For variation, some areas should be laid more heavily than others.

3 Once you have practised drawing bison shapes from a reference book onto paper first, draw them directly onto the wall with charcoal. Complete all the bison images you have chosen at this stage.

4 Use a dusting brush to dust away the excess charcoal.

TEXTURED SURFACES

Producing a dilapidated surface on a wall is a free and creative process. It's an ideal opportunity to experiment with different tones and consistencies of acrylic glaze. What may at first seem like apparent mistakes can turn into rugged relief later on. Vary the weight of pigment-tinted acrylic glaze in different areas to increase the irregularities. Paper and natural sponges may be used to produce fine textures. The deeper the density of the acrylic glaze, the deeper the resulting texture. As the layers are built up, interest is heightened and the depth strengthened.

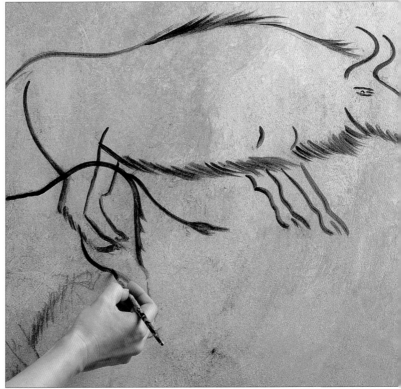

5 & 6 With dark brown and a medium-sized artist's brush, start to paint over the charcoaled lines. Continue to cover all the outlines of the bison with the same colour and brush.

YOU WILL NEED

Household
  brushes for
  preparation of
  wall
Newspaper
Natural sponge
Cave painting
  reference book
Charcoal
Dusting brush
Fine and
  medium-sized
  artist's brushes
Badger softener
Steel wool
12.5cm (5in)
  household
  brush
Basic equipment
  (see page 74)

7 With a burnt umber and burnt sienna mix, paint in some random cracks on the wall. To do this, work diagonally, varying the thickness of the lines.

8 Soften the cracks while they are still wet by working a dry dusting brush or badger softener from side to side over the top of them.

9 With steel wool, gently rub over the dark brown outlines of the bison to soften and distress them a little.

10 Now paint your fingertips with slightly diluted burnt sienna and drag them loosely down the wall.

11 Next, paint the entire inside of your hand with the same burnt sienna as step 10 and press your hand onto the wall to leave a bold caveman-like imprint.

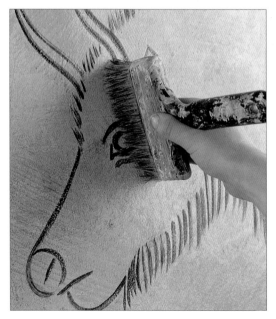

12 Finally, although not imperative, a third layer of thin raw umber acrylic glaze may be applied with a wide brush and this will increase the feeling of age and dilapidation.

Simple silhouettes

YOU WILL NEED

Household brushes for preparation of wall
Spirit level / Bubble level (for grid method)
Medium-sized fitch
2.5cm (1in) brush
Fine artist's brush
Basic equipment (see page 74)

Profiles are the simplest form of mural to achieve. With no shading or perspective to worry about, external form and outline are the only concern and blocking in in a single colour is swift and effective. Painted beside a fireplace, these life-size figures have a disarming impact. They stand as an amusing addition to a sparsely furnished room. Once the design was worked out on paper (see Step 1), the wall was prepared with cream matt emulsion (latex).

1 Design and draw your figures on paper first. Take books, magazines and real people for your inspiration. Complete accuracy is not necessary unless you decide to use the grid method (see page 77). Copy the figures by transferring them freehand to the wall in pencil. In this instance they vary a little in scale from the drawing.

2 With the outlines drawn in pencil, begin to block in the figure shapes with black paint. Use a medium-sized fitch to create the hard basic outline; the centres may be blocked in with a larger brush. Work on one figure at a time; start at the top and work downwards.

COLOUR PALETTE
You will need the colours below (see Paint Directory, pages 108–113).

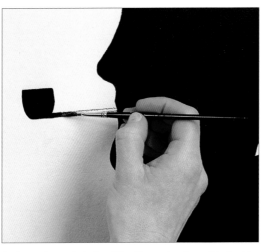

3 Once the main bulk of the figures has been blocked in, use a fine artist's brush to add in the more delicate areas, such as the pipe in this case.

4 Finally, the most delicate areas of the silhouette design, such as a feather, are completed with the smallest of artist's brushes.

Kilim painted floor

The combined order and passion achieved in kilim patterns and colours is a rare mixture. Their beauty is unpretentious and their appeal is bold and direct. This floor contains motifs that are fundamental to kilims, such as the lozenge and diamond. They provide a lively source of inspiration and form the basis of an effective design that works. A casual and informal room was in mind when this floor design was conceived. It sits comfortably beside an authentic kilim stool and natural terracotta tiles, where the elementary inspiration is apparent.

COLOUR PALETTE
You will need the colours below (see Paint Directory, pages 108–113).

Planning the design

Once the design was worked out on paper, the floor (made of MDF) was primed and prepared with terracotta matt emulsion (latex). The horizontal wide stripes were measured and drawn with soft pencil. They were taped with low-tack masking tape (see page 79) and painted in pale orange. The border lines around the edge were then drawn and painted in black using exactly the same method.

The remaining design was then measured and with soft pencil the correct positioning of the lines and shapes was deduced. Do not be disheartened by the amount of time this takes. Measuring out any project is laborious, but it is a vital part of the design process.

Once the scale had been established, six stencils were cut (see page 78). Again, do not be daunted by the amount of taping up and stencilling required. The most effective way of carrying out the work is to complete all the same coloured and same shaped stages at the same time.

Working on a flat floor surface as opposed to a wall makes holding the stencils in place considerably easier. To prevent smudging, apply adhesive spray to the back of the stencils to hold them temporarily in position. To achieve crisp lines, it is vital not to overload your brush with paint. Try to work in a neat and methodical manner and this project will be much easier to achieve. All the colours used for this project are inspired by traditional kilims. Their impressions are generally much stronger due to the lack of combined hues that often occur in the softened weave of the genuine article. The floor was left to dry and sealed with acrylic floor varnish (see page 76).

The final effect is simple although the work involved is considerable. A word of advice here: 'Do it, but choose a small room!' You will be thrilled with your results.

YOU WILL NEED

Household brushes for preparation of floor
Selection of 2.5cm (1in) brushes
Cutting mat
Stencil card
Scalpel
Adhesive spray (optional)
10cm (4in) glider (varnish brush)
Acrylic matt floor varnish
Basic equipment (see page 74)

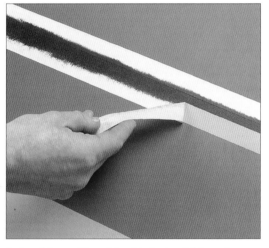

1 Pencil the position of the thin horizontal lines, then tape the lines on either side (see page 79). Stipple dark blue within the taped area. Here, the tape is carefully removed to reveal a faultlessly straight line.

2 Draw the position of the main lozenge shapes and tape the lines on either side (see page 79). Here, warm cream is stippled within the taped area. Try to keep your stippling as even as possible.

3 Begin stencilling with the largest stencil so that the overall design takes shape more quickly and is easier to visualize. Here, prussian blue is stencilled in between the lozenge shapes.

4 Once the larger motifs were complete, the Christmas tree shaped stencil was placed neatly in position as shown and stippled in an irresistible shade of green.

5 To save time, a row of stencils was cut to build up a line of them from one sheet of stencil card. Green, blue and warm cream motifs were applied. Here, a green motif is stippled.

6 Once the prussian blue shapes were dry (about 15 minutes), a diamond shaped stencil was centrally positioned and stippled with the terracotta in the same colour as the background.

7 Another diamond shaped stencil was then applied on top of the remaining alternate prussian blue shapes and stippled using the same dark blue as for the pale orange horizontal lines.

8 Finally, once the terracotta diamonds were dry (about 15 minutes), the smallest of the prepared stencils was positioned centrally and then stippled in dark blue. Leave the floor to dry thoroughly (24 hours, if possible) and seal with several coats of acrylic varnish for protection (see page 76).

Mock stone floor

Stone floors are timeless and work well throughout the home. This example of painted stone squares has a quiet and calming effect. The surrounding border and smaller squares, painted in dark green granite, add contrast and strength to the retiring stone. Easy to live with, this project is quick and simple to achieve.

COLOUR PALETTE
You will need the colours below (see Paint Directory, pages 108–113).

The design of the stone floor was first worked out on paper. Once this was established, the floor (made of MDF) was primed and then prepared with cream acrylic (latex) eggshell. When the paint was dry, the border and diagonally positioned stone squares were measured and drawn with soft pencil and a ruler. The central technique used on this floor is frottage (see page 82). Its effect has an organic feel, no two frottaged areas will ever be the same and it is rewardingly fast to achieve. Finally, the floor was left to dry and sealed with acrylic floor varnish (see page 76).

1 First, mix an acrylic glaze (see page 76) using yellow ochre and raw umber. Following the pencil lines, fill in the first square with glaze using a 2.5cm (1in) brush. Once the square is covered with glaze, immediately lay a sheet of newspaper across it. Gently stroke the back of the newspaper with a rag so that full contact is made, then remove it immediately as the glaze will dry quickly. Complete all the squares.

2 Use low-tack masking tape to create the grouting lines between squares. Each diagonal line should be taped from beginning to end. Here, the taped line is stippled with stone coloured matt emulsion (latex). Once each line is complete, remove the tape and move on to the next.

3 Cut a small square from stencil card (see page 78) in correct proportion to the size of the completed squares. Place the stencil in position and stipple the green base colour for the granite centre. Complete all the squares in this way and then paint the surrounding border at the edge of the floor with the same green base colour.

4 Once the paint is dry, tape around the edges of the central squares. Mix an acrylic glaze from Hooker's green and ivory black. Apply a top coat to the central squares using a 2.5cm (1in) brush. Here, the granite effect is carried out using the gentle dabbing motion of a sponge. Carefully remove the tape. Complete the remaining squares, then sponge the border in the same way. Leave the floor to dry thoroughly (24 hours, if possible) and seal with several coats of acrylic floor varnish for protection (see page 76).

Spaceship porthole

Looking out from your own spaceship with an industrial yellow and orange striped interior is a novel idea. The view from this porthole is of a 1950s-style rocket with a scattering of stars and a mysterious planet lurking nearby.

COLOUR PALETTE
You will need the colours below (see Paint Directory, pages 108–113).

Silver metallic paint and black are the predominant colours used in this project. The silver has been applied in three different ways: freehand, sprayed with an aerosol through a stencil and stippled through a stencil. These techniques are explained in the steps that follow.

Detailing on the rocket is highlighted by the use of red. This gives added strength to the three bolts on the porthole's interior. The addition of acrylic gloss varnish gives the illusion of glass.

Planning the design

This is a simple and straightforward image for a beginner to achieve. A strong yellow matt emulsion (latex) was first applied to the wall. The orange stripes were created with low-tack masking tape (see page 79) and a dustbin (garbage) lid was used to trace the outline of the porthole. Painted here within a windowless staircase, this idea works best where there is little natural light and it would be ideal for a child's basement den.

The pencil and string method (see step 3) is a useful way of creating the outer porthole circle. Stencils were cut during the planning stage (see page 78) and were held in position with spray mount. Metallic paints are widely available and extremely effective. They provide excellent coverage and give the appropriate outer space-like quality needed for this project.

1 Measure with a steel ruler and pencil and paint the diagonal stripes with the help of low-tack masking tape. Here, strident orange is stippled with a household brush.

2 A dustbin (garbage) lid is the perfect size for the inner circle of the porthole. Decide on your position and draw around it carefully with a pencil.

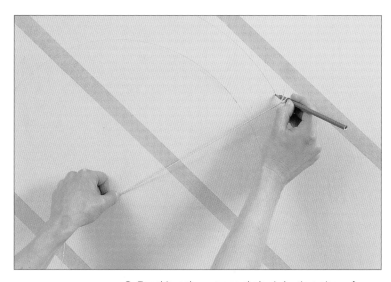

3 To achieve the outer porthole circle, tie a piece of string to a pencil and hold the string firmly in the centre with a drawing pin (tack) to keep it taut. Swing the pencil round to create the circle, then draw in the three outlines for the bolt holders with a ruler and soft pencil.

4 Block in the inner circle of the porthole with black matt emulsion (latex) and a glider (varnish brush).

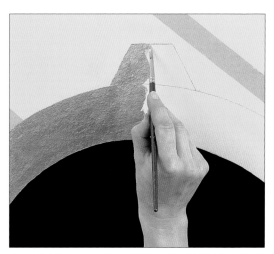

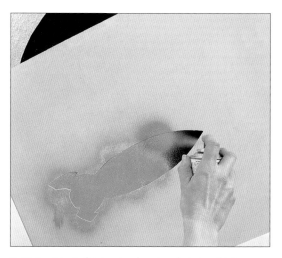

YOU WILL NEED

Household brushes for preparation of wall
Steel rule
Tracing paper
Cutting mat
Stencil card
Scalpel
Dustbin (garbage) lid
String
Drawing pin (tack)
2.5cm (1in) brush
5cm (2in) glider (varnish brush)
Fine and medium-sized artist's brushes
Silver metallic paint
Adhesive spray
Silver aerosol spray
Medium-sized fitch
Acrylic gloss varnish
Basic equipment (see page 74)

5 Now block in the frame to the porthole with silver metallic paint using a medium-sized artist's brush.

6 Spray mount the previously cut rocket stencil into position and spray it with a silver aerosol as shown.

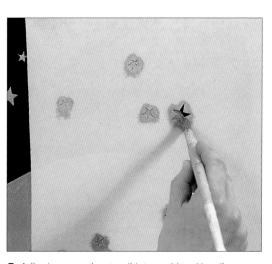

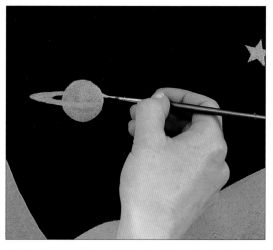

7 Adhesive spray the stencil into position. Use silver metallic paint and a fitch to stipple in the previously cut star stencils.

8 First draw and then paint in the planet freehand with silver metallic paint and a fine artist's brush.

A kick and a glow are added to your walls with metallic paints. The choice of shades is wide, with a broad selection available on the mar/metallic images of stars, planet and rocket sit together on the boundless black producing graphic and simplistic images.

9 Here, the rocket is given some red highlights. The three bolts are also painted in red at this stage.

10 Give extra definition to the inner edge of the porthole with a darker silver line.

11 Finally, apply a coat of acrylic gloss varnish to the central porthole to emphasize the illusion of glass.

Flower-strewn floor

This soft and gentle painted floor is ideal for a conservatory or sunny breakfast room. The asymmetric simple flower and leaf shapes are subtly balanced and complement each other well to give the impression of peaceful order. To create this project, the MDF floorboards were first primed and prepared with soft green matt emulsion (latex). Here, the correct background colour is a vital consideration: it needs to be neither too pale nor too dominant. The stencils were designed and cut (see page 78), with a satisfactory distinction of shapes achieved. A good contrast between the greens was chosen for the thorny leaves and tulip leaves.

YOU WILL NEED
Household brushes for preparing floor
Tracing paper
Cutting mat
Stencil card
Scalpel
2.5cm (1in) house hold brush
Fine, small and medium-sized artist's brushes
Acrylic floor varnish
10cm (4in) glider (varnish brush)
Basic equipment (see page 74)

Precise measurement of where the stencils were to be painted was unnecessary. The structure of the design was led by the larger of the two stencils. This was completed throughout the floor first and the smaller tulip fell into place automatically around it. Finally, the floor was left to dry and sealed with acrylic floor varnish (see page 76).

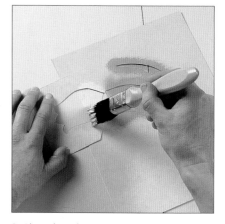

1 With the rough position of the stencils settled upon, stencil the largest of the two shapes in dark green. Stipple the centres of the leaves in a softer manner with a drier brush to create some light and variation. Complete all the intended leaf stencils to establish the basic framework of the design.

2 Place the tulip stencil in its position and stipple the stalk and leaves in a solid, paler shade of green. As shown, use another brush to carefully stipple the tulip heads in yellow. Complete the remaining tulip stencils.

COLOUR PALETTE
You will need the colours below (see Paint Directory, pages 108–113).

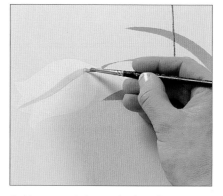

3 With the dark leaves now dry, apply the berries using a medium-sized artist's brush and a rich red. Clusters of berries are painted in the centres of the larger leaves and along the thorny stalks, with the odd one breaking away. Once they are dry, add a hint of light and reflection with a small artist's brush and the same milky-green colour as the overall background. One little sweep of a fine artist's brush in an arc shape completes this stage.

4 Here, a central curved stripe of stronger yellow is added to the tulip heads. This is a quick and easy way to increase the decorative dimension. Leave the floor to dry thoroughly (24 hours if possible) and seal with varnish for protection (see page 76).

COLOUR PALETTE
You will need white plus the colours below (see Paint Directory, pages 108–113).

Beyond the bath

This vibrant combination of blues, yellows, red and orange could enliven a dark, windowless bathroom. The scale of the mural is small and the content simple. Refreshing and clean-cut, the style and subject matter is almost certainly destined for a shower room, bathroom or even a swimming pool.

A cloudless sky and a waveless sea contribute to the design's graphic and direct appeal. The wash behind the boats and the gentle motion of the gull's wing are the only suggestion of movement. This is a bright and tranquil scene.

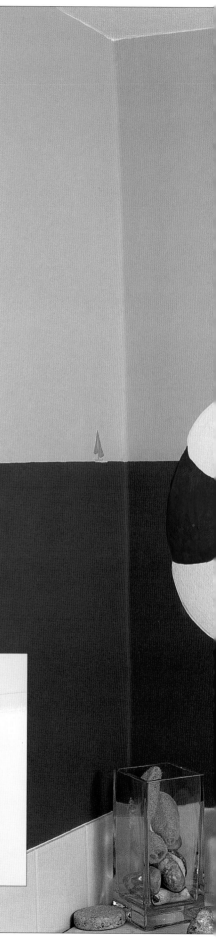

1 First, use a pencil and a spirit level (bubble level) to very lightly draw in the line of the horizon.

2 Boldly cut in the deep blue sea colour using a neat glider (varnish brush) with no straying hairs. Complete all the blocking in of the sea colour.

Planning the design

Next time you are at the seaside or any other wide open space, stand up straight and look at the horizon. You will notice that it is at eye level. Sit down, and the horizon sits down with you. From the top of the cliff or standing at the beach, the horizon is always at eye level. Decide from which viewpoint you will be looking at your mural for most of the time and strike that line at eye level. Plan your composition on paper.

Sky blue matt emulsion (latex) was used to block in the sky area (leave a rough edge just below eye level) and a deep blue was chosen for the sea. The lifebelt and post were added first, with boats completed last. In this mural, strength of colour is essential for the bold and sunny atmosphere.

YOU WILL NEED

Household brushes for preparation of wall
Spirit level (bubble level)
4cm (1½in) glider (varnish brush), 2.5cm (1in) brush, fine and medium artist's brushes
Natural history reference book
Palette
Cutting mat
Stencil card
Scalpel
Adhesive spray
Acrylic matt varnish
10cm (4in) glider (varnish brush)
Basic equipment (see page 74)

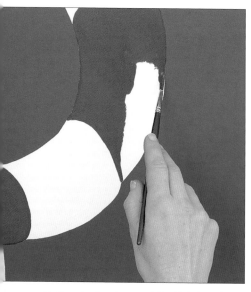

3 Draw in the shapes of the lifebelt and supporting post. Block them in in white and cream, and add the rounded ring stripes. Here, you see the last of the red rings being painted in with a medium-sized artist's brush and strong red.

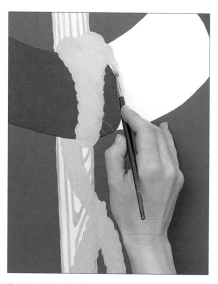

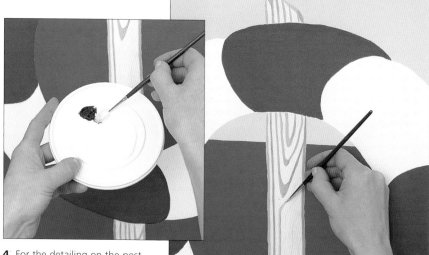

4 For the detailing on the post, mix raw umber and white acrylics together with a fine artist's brush. First draw in the stylized wood grain lines of the post and then, working from the top downwards, simply follow the lines and paint them in.

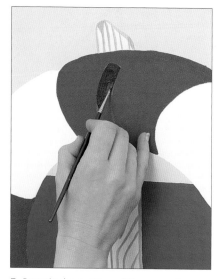

5 Draw in the position of the supporting hook and then boldly apply raw umber with an artist's brush.

6 Now draw in the outline of the coiled rope and block it in with a rich sand colour.

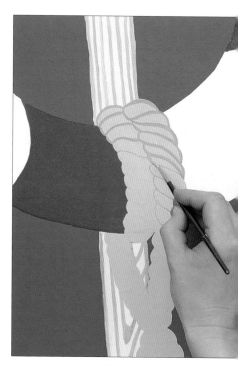

7 To create the detailing on the rope, first draw in the strands of rope and then paint over your lines with a deeper yellow sand.

8 Having found the inspiration for your desired gull shape in a bird book or at the seaside, draw it out on paper. Trace the outline onto stencil card and cut it out. Appropriately position the stencil with spray mount and stipple it in white with a 2.5cm (1in) household brush.

CLOUDS AND WAVES

Elemental effects, such as wind, waves and clouds, would spoil the character of this calm scene. For more spirited beach scenes, increase the tempo with turbulant clouds and rippling waves. Introduce naive cottonwool clouds with stencils; looser natured ones are achieved with acrylic glazed ragging and softening (see page 14). A suggestion of waves and foam may be sponged with diluted white emulsion (latex).

9 Draw in the shape of the gull's feet and then paint the beak and the feet in vivid orange.

10 Return to your source of inspiration and draw in the gull's eye and add some definition to the wings. Follow your pencil lines and paint them with a pale grey.

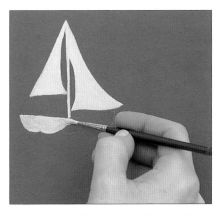

11 Draw the sails, mast and first boat shape amidst the deep blue sea. Paint the mast and sails in yellow.

12 Now paint the base of the boat in blue and complete the horizon, sails and masts in a deeper yellow.

13 Add a suggestion of wave to the base of the boat with a wash line running behind. Complete the remaining boats using the same method. When the wall is dry, apply several coats of acrylic matt varnish to protect it from splashes of water and steam.

Outside-in

The idea of looking into a window from the dark outside is depicted less often than the more conventional scene of a light interior window looking out onto a sunny green vista. This bright, sharp mural, inspired by a painting by the British artist, Patrick Caulfield, represents clarity itself – no clutter, no wiggly lines, no grey areas and certainly no curtains. The hard, graphic lines and stark colours are punchy, acute and amazingly simple to achieve. For this project, choose an awkward wall at the end of a corridor or at the side of a staircase.

Prepare your wall with black matt emulsion (latex). With a spirit level (bubble level) and white soluble crayon, draw in the outline of the window. (This one is roughly 61 x 90cm/2 x 3ft.) Apply low-tack masking tape to the outside edge of the window and block in the centre with a strong orange matt emulsion (latex). Remove the tape to reveal the crisp lines. Practise drawing the hanging light, radio and pencils in pot shapes on paper first and pencil them in position.

Then with a spirit level (bubble level), draw in the lines that suggest the ceiling, corner of the room and window crossbars.

YOU WILL NEED
Household brushes for preparation of wall
Spirit level (bubble level)
White soluble crayon
Fine and medium-sized artist's brushes
Fitch
Basic equipment (see page 74)

COLOUR PALETTE
You will need the colours below (see Paint Directory, pages 108–113).

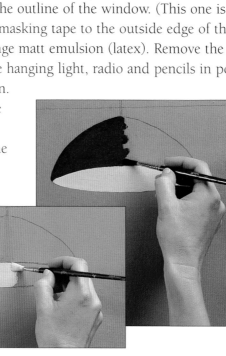
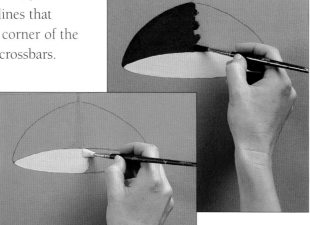

1 With a medium-sized artist's brush, block in the pale yellow section of the hanging light. Now use the same brush to carefully block in the strong blue of the shade.

2 With a fine artist's brush, apply the black outline of the light for extra definition.

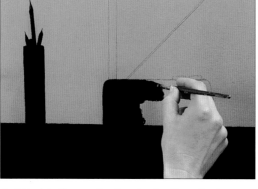

3 Complete the pencil pot and radio silhouettes by blocking them in neatly with black.

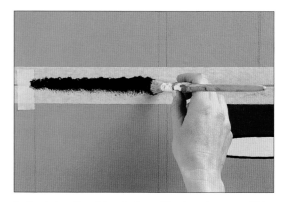

4 Apply lengths of low-tack masking tape (see page 79) to the interior lines that suggest the ceiling and corner of the room. Stipple these in black with a fitch. Complete the mural by painting the line that supports the light and the window crossbars using the same low-tack masking tape technique as before.

TROMPE
L'OEIL

Trompe trickery

The art of trompe l'oeil has a long and honourable tradition. The quest for depicting reality has been around ever since stone age man stuck his finger in some wet earth and drew a circle on the wall of his cave. The Ancient Greeks celebrated an artist whose depictions of fruit were so realistic that the birds flew down to peck at them and the artists of the Italian Renaissance devoted themselves to glorifying Nature's work in all its beauty.

The perfect trompe l'oeil goes unnoticed and is taken to be reality. As a rule, you should try to paint the objects life-size. It is important to place a trompe l'oeil painting in an appropriate spot; for example, the hooks holding a set of keys and the dog lead by the back door (see pages 50–3) and the string of chilli peppers close to the work surface in the kitchen (see pages 60–1).

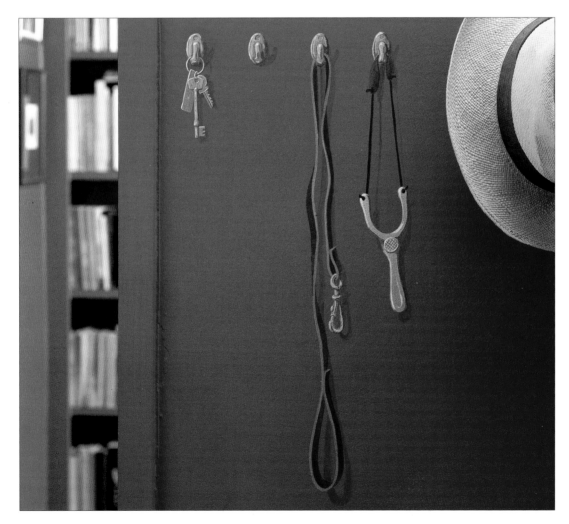

This detail (above) from the Rose Trellis Arch trompe l'oeil allows a closer look at the varied textures within the painting. There is the rough stipple of the foreground wall, the denser stipple of the grass, the soft treatment of the flagstones and the patchy sponge on the hedge beyond.

Apart from being used to paint keys and dog leads on hooks (left), this style of trompe l'oeil lends itself to the depiction of some rather more eccentric items that are personal to you or your family. Always remember to keep your images life-size – the reality will fall apart if you don't.

When you are trying to depict reality, you should be aware that you cannot possibly paint every subtle change of tone, speck of colour or blade of grass. The painter's job is to imitate. It is what you leave out and what you invite the viewer to fill in for you that creates the illusion. Many people get very anxious about perspective but there is no need to worry about it here. In the following examples, the depth is conveyed by shadow and highlight, and not by geometry.

The varied projects in this section are all chosen to help you master some of the basic tricks of the trade. Whether you are depicting the rough stone texture of the chunk of masonry or the shiny brass of the key (see pages 48–9 and 50–3), the effects are all achieved with just a brush and some paint. The techniques are the same but it's how you apply them that creates the magic. Don't be frightened of making mistakes: they are there to be learnt from. Remember, it is only paint and you can always exploit any accidents or simply paint them out and then start again.

The small scale of this trompe (left) should encourage complete beginners. These chillis amuse the eye and could make a discreet and rather engaging addition to the batterie de cuisine.

The dramatic drape (above) is easier than it looks. Once the drawing is on the wall and you've mastered painting the stripes, what follows is merely repetition. Shadows and highlights fall into place around the stripes.

Fragment of masonry

This crumbling architectural trompe has an unerring reality about it. The illusion of weight is almost daunting. Hung high on the wall, its presence is informal and quite splendid. For a grander look (and a longer job), the same technique may be applied to a cornice around a whole room. Large amounts of application and methodical work are required, but the results are sensational.

YOU WILL NEED
Household
  brushes to
  prepare board
MDF cut to size
Jigsaw
Sandpaper
Palette
10cm (4in)
  dusting brush
Fine and
  medium-sized
  artist's brushes
Medium fitch
Basic equipment
  (see page 74)

COLOUR PALETTE
You will need white plus the colours below (see Paint Directory, pages 108–113).

Any design of architectural detail may be used for this project. This one is adapted from a photo-graph of a cornice seen in a magazine. Classical Roman mouldings are used, with the row of small blocks resembling teeth, known as dentils, providing the finer detail.

First draw a basic shape on MDF and cut it out with a jigsaw, working the blade carefully to produce rough and uneven edges. Sand the edges to give a smooth, weathered look and then prepare the surface with a dirty, off-white vinyl silk emulsion satin (latex) base.

1 First, carefully rule the horizontal lines and details in pencil. Draw a rough line on the right-hand side to form the broken edge. Mix up a thin raw umber acrylic glaze and keep some undiluted raw umber handy on a palette. Paint on the acrylic glaze, adding solid colour here and there. Stipple the acrylic glaze roughly using a dusting brush. The pattern of broken colour needs to be kept irregular and patchy. With a medium-sized artist's brush and raw umber, pull a jagged line or two across the stone area to form cracks. Thicken the line randomly and unevenly as shown.

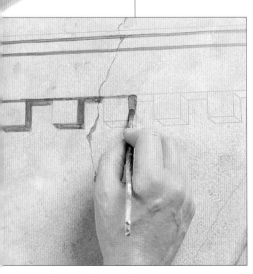

2 Use a slightly thinned raw umber to carefully paint in the hard shadows around the square dentils.

3 With a shadow acrylic glaze and a touch of the thinned off-white base colour, paint in the softer shadows and highlight the curved moulding with a fitch. Use the shadow acrylic glaze to apply a little soft shadow to the dentil's flat surface and on the smaller moulding beneath.

4 To complete the aged effect, add highlights to the cracks with the same colour as the base and a fine artist's brush.

Hang it all

This little trompe is a charmer. Virtually every house-hold has a place for a row of hooks; they can nestle in a hallway, by the back door, almost unnoticed until someone tries to walk the dog. Pictured here in the corner of a red hallway, their presence is discreet and the catapult introduces a more interesting shape and subject beside the more day-to-day images of keys and a dog lead. The beauty of this kind of trompe is that you can let yourself go and depict your own choice of things to hang from the hooks, from the sweetly mundane to the mysteriously personal. Choose your objects, hang them from a hook and draw them life size. You may prefer to take a photograph; sometimes it's easier to copy from than the real thing. As ever with trompe l'oeil, the more appropriate the objects depicted are to the site, the more complete the final illusion will be.

Planning the design

Some accurate drawing and considerable care is required for this project, but it's worth it. Experiment on paper until you are satisfied with the scale and shape of your objects. Be aware of where the real light falls across the wall and where the real shadows of door frames and suchlike would fall. Let reality enhance and compliment your illusion, not fight it. A white soluble crayon is used to transfer the design onto the wall. This shows up well against a strong background and disappears into the paint when you start colouring it with water-based acrylics.

The wall was first prepared with a deep red emulsion (latex) and fine and medium-sized artist's brushes were used throughout the steps.

COLOUR PALETTE
You will need white plus the colours below (see Paint Directory, pages 108–113).

1 Once you are satisfied with your design, copy it life-size in white crayon directly onto the wall.

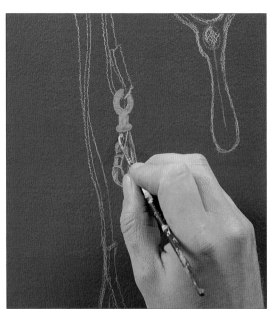

2 With a fine artist's brush, block in all the brass elements in a base coat of yellow ochre.

YOU WILL NEED
Household brushes for preparation of wall
White water-soluble crayon
Fine and medium-sized artist's brushes
Basic equipment (see page 74)

HIGHLIGHTS AND SHADOW ON METAL SURFACES

When painting metal, remember that as a shiny surface, it reflects what is around it. This means highlights and shadow. After drawing the shape, paint in the base colour; in this case, the yellow ochre colour of brass over the whole area. On one side, paint a burnt sienna shadow, following the contours of the shape, leaving a hard edge on both sides. On the opposite side, paint a band of whitened yellow ochre, similarly following the contours of the object, varying the width to mimic the imperfections of the metal. On top of this, a fine line of white can be painted to give a little sparkle to catch the eye.

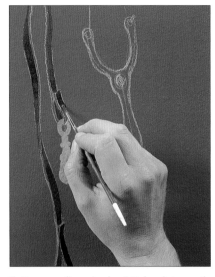

3 Use a medium-sized artist's brush to neatly block in the leather part of the dog lead in burnt umber.

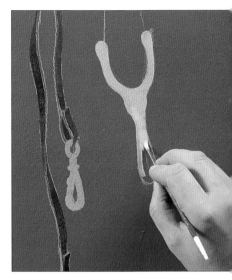

4 Now carefully block in the catapult in a light shade of grey.

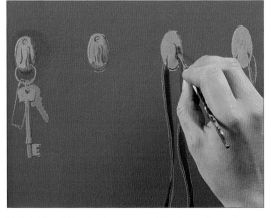

5 Paint in all the shadow areas of the brass elements with burnt sienna.

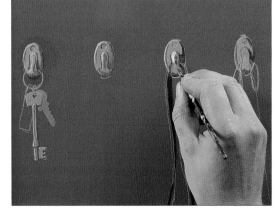

6 With a mix of white and yellow ochre, add highlights to the brass elements.

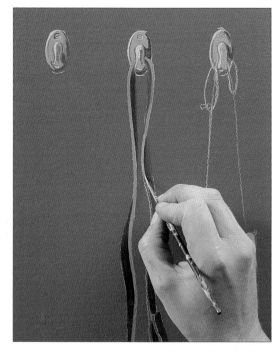

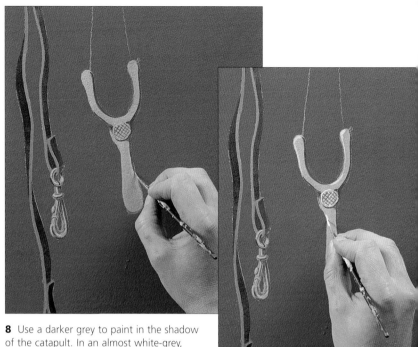

7 Now paint in the edge of the trailing dog lead neatly with raw sienna.

8 Use a darker grey to paint in the shadow of the catapult. In an almost white-grey, paint in the highlight and then the detailing on the catapult.

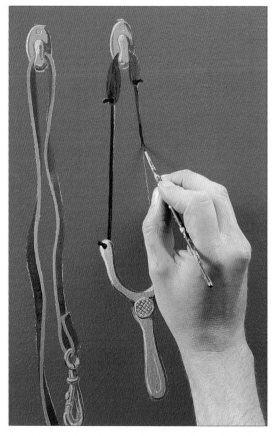

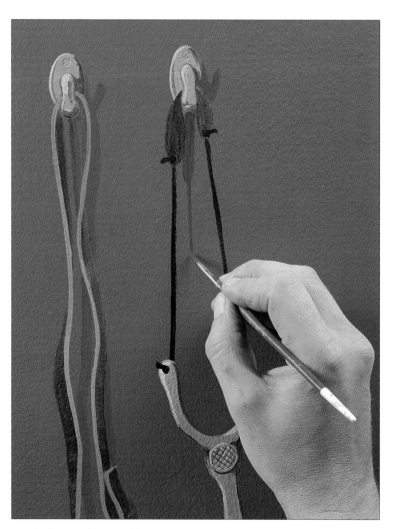

9 With some Payne's grey and burnt umber, paint in the elastic and sling of the catapult.

10 Finally, use a burnt umber acrylic glaze to paint in the shadows cast by all the objects on the wall.

Plate in a grate

The firescreen is an old idea that goes back at least a couple of hundred years. For this project, you will need to select a fairly strong shape and an image that could believably sit in such a space. In this case, a large china plate has been chosen, but it could equally be a tray, an urn or even a pile of books.

On a board cut to the exact size of the opening, paint a mid-grey matt emulsion (latex) base coat and draw in the basic design of the plate and the space behind it. The depth of this space is conveyed through the structural lines within the fireplace and from the shadow thrown to the side and top of the overmantel.

YOU WILL NEED

Household brushes for preparation of MDF
Piece of MDF, cut to size with a jigsaw
Large fitch
Fine and medium-sized artist's brushes
Basic equipment (see page 74)

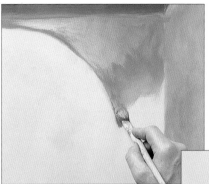

1 With a large fitch, paint in the dark grey shadows thrown by the sides of the mantel up to the edge of the plate. Soften the edges into the lighter grey base. Paint in the shadow cast by the plate, angling the shape where it falls across the corner and onto the floor.

COLOUR PALETTE
You will need white plus the colours below (see Paint Directory, pages 108–113).

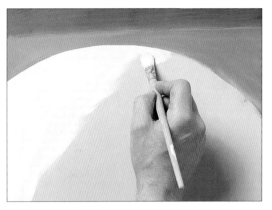

2 Now paint in the base colour of the plate with a very pale green. If necessary, use a smaller brush for this job as it is important to keep a crisp edge here.

3 With a medium-sized artist's brush, paint in the blue border around the outer edge and the inner circle of the plate. Draw in the main pattern very lightly in pencil. With a fine artist's brush, paint in the green leafy design and then add the blue berries to complete the effect.

4 Mix a shadow acrylic glaze with Payne's grey. Brush it lightly at the top and to the left of the inner circle.

5 Finally, add an almost-white highlight to the outer rim and the bottom right of the inner circle.

Theatrical drape

This sumptuous example of a draped curtain is full of dramatic flourish and gusto. Loosely hung over a brass rail and held back by a solid brass boss, it is painted beside the large bay window of a drawing room.

To render the weight and elegance of a heavy swathe of fabric can at first appear to be a daunting and difficult task, but if you follow the steps then you should be able to produce an impressive image fairly quickly. Like everything else, practice makes better, if not perfect.

Planning the design

First, prepare the wall with a warm sand matt emulsion (latex) and use a deeper tone of acrylic (latex) eggshell on the skirting (baseboard). Before picking up a pencil, throw a tablecloth (or any other heavy fabric) over a chair, arrange the folds a little and look hard at how the fabric breaks and hangs. Do a few sketches on paper of the curved and angular shapes you see. After a little practice, take some charcoal and experiment on the wall. The most important thing to remember is to be brave: use your whole arm, not just your wrists, to achieve those big arcs. Once your confidence has built up, draw the outline of the drape onto the wall.

Painting a striped material rather than a plain one is considerably easier. Stripes help to express the fullness of the fabric; without them, all the suggestion of depth and solidity is dependant on your shading and highlighting. Let the stripes do all the hard work for you.

In this project, the direction of the falling light is an important consideration. For example, if you decide to paint the drapes to the right and left of a real window, the light will come between them and it will be thrown in opposite directions for each drape. Here, the draped curtain is painted on the right of the actual window and the shadows and highlights have been painted accordingly.

In this detail, you can see some of the movement and depth created by the stripes on the curtain. Held in place by a brass boss, this part is more like a conventional curtain. If you took the boss away, the folds would just fall across the width of the window.

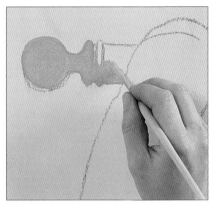

1 Relax and draw in the drapery with charcoal. Do not worry about whether that curve of fabric would really fall in that way as lines can be rectified later, if necessary.

2 Draw in the brass rail and, using a small fitch, paint it in yellow ochre. The boss may be drawn and painted using the same colours at this stage.

CREATING FOLDS

When trying to create the illusion of heavy folds of fabric, it's tempting to think of parallel lines curving predictably around whatever object they are draped over. In reality, if you look at a swathe of fabric hanging across a line or thrown over a chair, the patterns are fairly chaotic and mixed. Fabric breaks in straight lines and long curves, doubling up into hills and valleys, and leaving expanses of flat prairie.

Essentially, it's about shape and shadow: the highlights are almost optional. Practise drawing a napkin hanging off the tablecloth, then expand to the tablecloth. There are endless types of folds, all of them unique. Theatrical and bold, striking and satisfying to draw and paint, this drape is just one example.

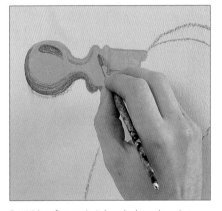

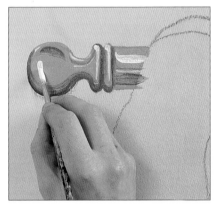

3 With a fine artist's brush, loosely paint burnt sienna in a broad stripe beneath the halfway point of the rail and then add a stripe near the top.

4 Now add some highlights to the rail with a little white tinted with a tiny amount of yellow ochre.

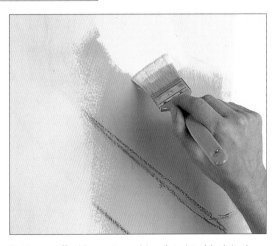

5 Use an off-white matt emulsion (latex) to block in the background to the drape with a household brush. The charcoal lines for the folds remain visible.

6 Draw in the stripes with charcoal. Although this will appear difficult at first, with practice it all begins to flow. Sometimes you actually have to cheat a little to make sense of the next step. This is perfectly acceptable and to be encouraged. Remember: you are creating a dramatic effect and no one will be checking details with a ruler.

YOU WILL NEED

Household
  brushes for
  preparation of
  wall
Charcoal
Small fitch
Fine artist's
  brush
Basic equipment
  (see page 74)

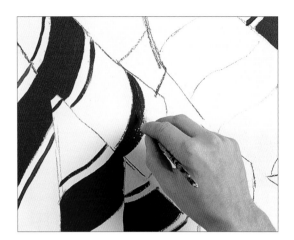

7 With an artist's brush, paint the wide stripes with a burnt sienna matt emulsion (latex). To enhance the overall pattern, add a thinner line each side of the stripes.

8 Mix a thin acrylic glaze with Payne's grey. This should be dark enough to register, but also transparent so the painting beneath it shows through. With the same brush as step 7, paint up to the edge of the fold. Now paint the majority of the shadow on one side of the drape; this will push the billows in the fabric forward.

10 Paint in the highlight on the billowed fabric using a fitch and a white-tinted glaze. Begin by painting the lines about 2.5cm (1 inch) in from the leading edge of each section. The larger the billow, the wider the highlight needs to be.

9 Mix a darker acrylic glaze with a little more Payne's grey. Use a smaller brush to work into the areas of shadow close to the line of the folds. This helps to accentuate the modelling and enhance the feeling of solidity.

11 Finally, use the same Payne's grey glaze to paint around the outside edges of the curtain, boss and beneath the rail. Remember that the right-hand side of the curtain casts a deeper shadow on the wall.

Red hot chilli peppers

YOU WILL NEED

Household brushes for preparation of wall

Fine and medium-sized artist's brushes

Basic equipment (see page 74)

COLOUR PALETTE
You will need white plus the colours below (see Paint Directory, pages 108–113).

These chilli peppers can add a little bite and warmth to the clean, antiseptic walls of a contemporary kitchen, or an extra glow to a traditional one. There is no substitute for drawing a couple of real chillis at different angles until you get a feel for the way they look. Painted with precision and done with a bare minimum of colours and steps, this is a relatively simple trompe, but no less effective for all of that.

The small scale of this piece makes it easy to live with. Teasingly realistic, the chillis can hang in a corner of your kitchen and tantalize you when you realize the one ingredient needed in your spicy pasta sauce is a red chilli.

Upheaval and disruption is absent when painting such a minute trompe. With a mere five colours, a dust sheet or drop cloth is hardly needed. A couple of concentrated hours, some chilli inspiration and the steps that follow should do the trick. The wall was first prepared with an off-white emulsion (latex). Use a medium-sized artist's brush throughout for the steps unless otherwise indicated.

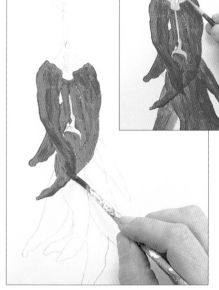

1 Once you have drawn the chillis, nail and string in outline directly on the wall, block in the chillis with acra red. Then block in the colour of the string and the chilli stalks in a mix of yellow ochre, raw umber and white.

2 With a cadmium red and burnt umber mix, darken the right-hand side of the chillis. Use a whirling motion to work your brush into the left side here and there to give that gnarled, dried-out feel. Paint in the details of the stalks and string with a finer brush. Add a little more burnt umber to your mix from the previous step and shade one side.

3 Following the rounded, gnarled shapes previously made with the darker red (see step 2), add a few more white highlights to the chillis with the same brush.

4 Finally, mix a transparent shadow glaze and carefully paint in the shadow around the chillis and string.

Rose trellis arch

Capture the tranquillity and light of a summer afternoon with this pretty rural scene. Impressionistic in style, when painted on a kitchen wall or at the end of a long corridor, it provides a relaxing and welcome escape from the reality and rigours of everyday life. The structural archway and trellis, softened by climbing roses, frame the view beyond. A flagstone path draws the eye towards the focal point of the fountain and its dancing water to increase the illusion of depth.

COLOUR PALETTE
You will need white plus the colours below (see Paint Directory, pages 108–113).

Planning the design

It is most important to study the real thing before you start this project. Look at the shape of a rose bush, its stems and leaves; observe the way flagstones can be laid, and so on. If you are able to capture a sense of reality in your initial drawing, the subsequent painting will be so much better. The wall was first prepared with a soft white matt emulsion (latex). With the exception of the rose bushes, which are added later, all the outlines are drawn boldly on the wall with charcoal. Remember to brush away the excess before you begin to paint.

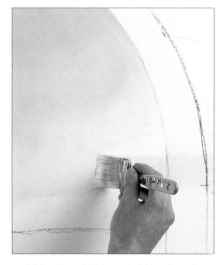

1 With a 5cm (2in) household brush, paint in the summer sky beneath the arch. Put some ultramarine and white on a palette. Use the white to lighten the bottom of the sky and soften it into the pale blue mix at the top.

2 Block in the hedge with a light permanent green and white mix. Leave a ragged edge at the top and bottom and let this dry.

3 With a natural sponge and some pure light permanent green, dab on a broken colour texture over the hedge.

YOU WILL NEED

Household
 brushes for
 preparation of
 wall
Charcoal
5cm (2in) house-
 hold brush
Natural sponge
Medium-sized
 artist's brush
Medium-sized
 fitch
Basic equipment
 (see page 74)

4 Using the same green, block in the grassy areas. While they are still wet, stipple the grass with a household brush to introduce a little texture.

5 Block in the base colour for the flagstones with a thinned mixture of raw umber and white (add water). Leave this patchy with the charcoal showing through.

6 With some pure raw umber and a medium-sized artist's brush, follow the charcoal lines beneath and paint in the cracks between the flagstones. Don't be too precise: the cracks should vary in thickness. Once the cracks are dry, darken some of the slabs with the thin base colour of raw umber and white.

7 Apply low-tack masking tape in a trellis pattern to the two rectangular areas on either side of the archway. Then roughly stipple a burnt umber and white mix over the whole wall area with a 5cm (2in) household brush.

8 Now gently remove the tape to reveal the regular diamond pattern of white trellis.

9 To paint the inside of the arch, use the burnt umber mix on the right and blend it into a much lighter raw umber and white mix on the left.

10 First draw in the roses with a soft pencil. Remember to group the leaves in clusters of five. Paint the stems (above) with a medium-sized artist's brush and burnt umber. The leaves are painted in sap green (opposite).

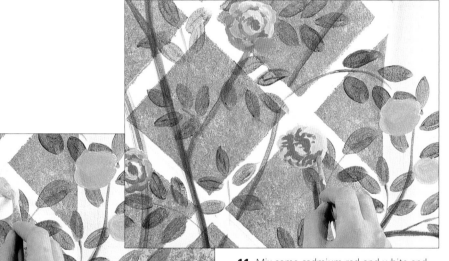

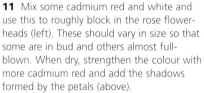

11 Mix some cadmium red and white and use this to roughly block in the rose flower-heads (left). These should vary in size so that some are in bud and others almost full-blown. When dry, strengthen the colour with more cadmium red and add the shadows formed by the petals (above).

12 First block in the shape of the fountain with raw umber and a little white. Keep the left-hand side a little denser in colour to indicate the shadow and leave to dry. Here, the colour is first lightened with white and then applied to create highlights on the right.

13 With a fitch and some sap green, stipple the plants and shrubs beneath the hedge. Then, using an artist's brush, add occasional little tufts of grass beneath the flagstones.

14 Now add the dancing water of the fountain with some pure titanium white.

15 Finally, paint in the shadow on the flagstones to the left of the fountain with a thin raw umber mix. Spend some time going over the whole painting to tidy up any rough edges and tweak things here and there.

Gothic cubes

COLOUR PALETTE
You will need
white plus the
colours below (see
Paint Directory,
pages 108–113).

YOU WILL NEED
Household
  brushes for
  preparation of
  wall
Plumb line
  (optional)
2.5cm (1in)
  household
  brush
Square-headed
  fitch
Basic equipment
  (see page 74)

Dominant and exciting, this trompe l'oeil is inspired by some 16th-century wall paintings in a Danish medieval castle. The pattern of cubes in three colours – dark, medium and light – is a basic design and remarkably simple to accomplish. With its bold use of colour and strident effect, this style of trompe l'oeil would work best in a corridor or hallway.

Plan your design on paper first and prepare the wall with sand matt emulsion using a household brush. In this project, no acrylic pigments are needed: all three colours used to form the cubes are matt emulsion (latex).

1 With a large household brush, prepare the wall first with a base of sand coloured matt emulsion (latex). This will materialize into the left hand plane of the cubes.

2 Carefully measure and mark the necessary horizontal and vertical points for your desired cubes. A plumb line may be used to check the vertical points are in line. With a pencil and ruler, join the relevant points to form the structure of your cubes.

USING A PLUMB LINE

When measuring and marking the grid for the cubes on the wall, a plumb line will enable you to check that your vertical lines are straight. If you don't have a plumb line, make your own with a length of string and tie a weighty object, such as a pebble, to it.

3 Apply low-tack masking tape to the surrounds of each of the cubes that are to be painted in the strong blue. Block in the first cube with a small household brush (2.5cm/1in). Carefully remove the tape and complete the remaining blue cubes with the same method.

4 Finally, apply low-tack masking tape to the surrounds of the top of the cubes that are to be painted in white. Block in the area of the first cube using a square-headed fitch. Remove the tape and complete all the others with the same method. Once the cubes are complete, paint the skirting board (baseboard) and door with a dark red acrylic (latex) eggshell.

Fly the flags

This small painting is ideal for a child's bedroom and could be painted in their favourite team colours above a bed or desk. It uses some basic techniques that can be applied to a whole range of trompe l'oeil ideas. The principles are the same whether applied to these small pennants or to full-scale flags fluttering in the breeze. The small size and symmetry of this design will fit easily into any scheme and breathe life into the darkest corner of the room. Use bold colours and distinctive patterns to proudly announce your allegiance and fly the flags for your team.

Planning the design

Little disruption is caused when painting a trompe l'oeil on such a small scale. Take the phone off the hook, have a steadying cup of coffee, throw down the dust sheets, take a deep breath and launch into the drawing. By the end of the day, you could have transformed a small part of someone's den. Here, a broad pattern has been used but the same principles apply to any team colours. Tracing paper was useful for creating the symmetrical image on the wall (see page 77). The tracing was used again to draw in the shadows in step 13. This is a good time-saving device that can be applied to any complicated pattern. In this case, the wall was prepared with a soft cream matt emulsion (latex) and the design was perfected on paper first.

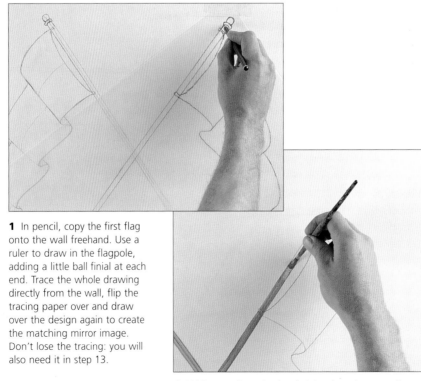

1 In pencil, copy the first flag onto the wall freehand. Use a ruler to draw in the flagpole, adding a little ball finial at each end. Trace the whole drawing directly from the wall, flip the tracing paper over and draw over the design again to create the matching mirror image. Don't lose the tracing: you will also need it in step 13.

2 With a medium-sized artist's brush and some yellow ochre, paint in the flagpoles.

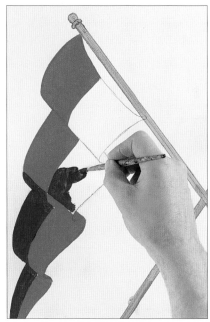

3 Now paint the base colours of the flag with cadmium red and ultramarine blue. Remember to curl the pattern around the falling folds.

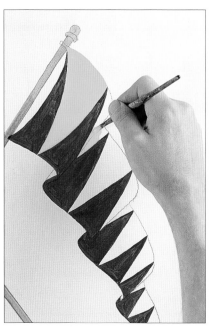

4 With the same brush, apply blue and cadmium yellow to the other flag.

5 Mix some Payne's grey with acrylic glaze and carefully paint the shadow alongside the fold. As you do this, always remember where the light is coming from.

6 Now use a palette with the three base colours and white. First mix the blue and white to add the highlight to the edge of the fold with a fine artist's brush.

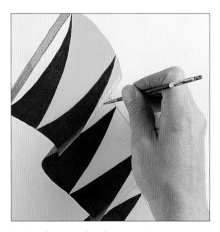

7 Use the same brush as step 6 to repeat the careful procedure with the yellow base colour and white.

8 Next, paint in the highlight with a red and white mix to the back of the fold on the left-hand flag.

9 Add some burnt umber to the yellow ochre and then apply a shadow to the two flagpoles.

10 With some white and a little yellow ochre, add in the highlight to the poles.

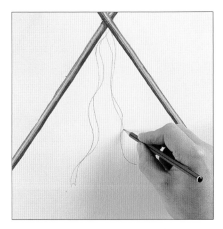

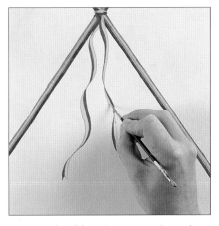

11 In pencil, draw some trailing ribbons to tie the two poles together.

12 Paint the ribbons in a contrasting red and yellow with an artist's brush to achieve a precise finish.

13 Retrieve the tracing that you used earlier and position it below and slightly to the left of the two flags. Lightly trace the bottom lines of the flags and poles to give an edge to the shadow.

14 Finally, mix a thin acrylic glaze of burnt umber and a little white, and paint the shadow below the flags, using the traced lines of step 13. Don't forget to add shadows to the ribbons.

FLAGS AND RIBBONS

When painting fluttering flags and ribbons, many of the same tricks that are used for drapery can be applied. Let your pencil draw a continuous series of 'S' shapes to create the regular folds of these pennants. To achieve the twisting ribbon shapes, draw a wavy vertical line and then almost repeat it in parallel, but crossing over the first line here and there. Remember that sometimes you will only see the edge of the ribbon, sometimes the full width. When adding the stripe of colour, follow the lines you have drawn and bring the colour to a point where it crosses over itself. The freer you are, the more movement will be introduced.

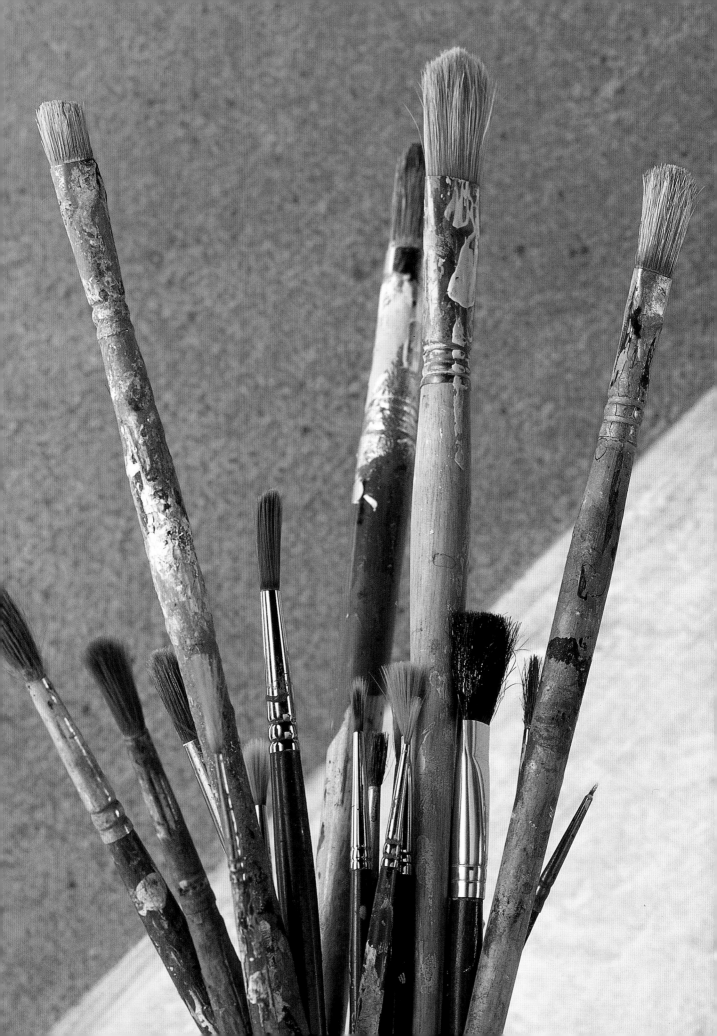

PRACTICAL
ADVICE

Planning and equipment

The preparation of your wall paves the way. Walls previously painted in water-based paint should be rubbed down with sandpaper and any holes or cracks filled with filler (spackle). Rub the walls down again and paint them with a coat of white matt emulsion (latex). Then paint at least two coats of your base colour: matt emulsion (latex) for most murals and trompes and vinyl silk emulsion (satin latex), with its mid-sheen finish, where acrylic glaze is to be applied.

For walls previously painted in an oil-based paint, a priming undercoat will be necessary so that the water-based matt emulsion (latex) adheres properly. Some walls may have been wallpapered. If the paper is loose, it needs to be stripped, rubbed down and prepared in the normal way. But if the wallpaper is firmly secured to the wall, you are in luck as matt emulsion (latex) can be applied directly to the surface to block it in straightaway.

Floorboards need to be thoroughly sanded and rubbed down to remove varnish or wax, then primed with an acrylic wood primer. Base coats can then be applied. Matt emulsion (latex) or acrylic eggshell (latex) are both appropriate here. Due to its toughness, acrylic latex eggshell

BASIC EQUIPMENT

The following is a list of equipment needed for creating the murals and trompe l'oeil demonstrations in this book:

- ◆ Pencil
- ◆ Eraser
- ◆ Charcoal
- ◆ White water-soluble crayon
- ◆ Drawing paper
- ◆ Newspaper
- ◆ Tracing paper
- ◆ Stencil card
- ◆ Cutting mat
- ◆ Scalpel
- ◆ Spray adhesive
- ◆ String and drawing pin (thumb tack)
- ◆ 91.5cm (three foot) long steel rule
- ◆ Step ladder
- ◆ Spirit level (bubble level)
- ◆ Low-tack masking tape
- ◆ Steel wool
- ◆ Natural sponge
- ◆ Household brushes
- ◆ Artist's brushes
- ◆ Fitches
- ◆ Gliders (varnish brushes)
- ◆ Dusting brush
- ◆ Wire brush
- ◆ Muslin rag
- ◆ Paint kettles and palettes
- ◆ Dust sheets/drop cloths

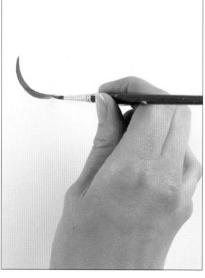

Artist's brushes
For adding that special highlight or the dot of a detail, keep a small selection of artist's brushes. Available in a variety of sizes and shapes, they are a constant companion to the trompe l'oeil projects in this book.

Fitches
Fitches are durable brushes. With a high bristle content, they hold a decent amount of paint and are delicate enough to allow you to carry out quite detailed work. Round, square and angled ends are available.

Clockwise from right: 10cm (4in) badger softener; selection of fitches, 2.5cm (1in) glider (varnish brush), 2.5cm (1in) household brush, 10cm (4in) dusting brush, fine and medium artist's brushes, natural sponge.

should be used as the base coat whenever acrylic glaze is to be applied. Floors with newly secured MDF are first primed with an acrylic primer and prepared in the normal way. Once the design is complete, several coats of acrylic floor varnish must be applied.

Brushes are versatile creatures and less than a dozen would be adequate to accomplish the projects described in this book. The more you become familiar with their particular foibles and strengths, the more you will enjoy them. Every painter has their favourite brush.

Small household brushes, fitches and gliders (varnish brushes) can often double up and share the same jobs. A dusting brush can stand as a passable badger softener for softening textured glazes and as it reaches middle age, can retire gracefully into an effective stippling brush.

A 91.5cm (3 foot) long ruler is needed for measuring and it is a good idea to keep a spirit level (bubble level) handy for checking vertical and horizontal lines. You will also require a scalpel to keep that pencil sharp and to cut stencils from waxed stencil card. Adhesive spray may be used to secure larger stencils to the wall, while low-tack masking tape will hold smaller ones in position.

Charcoal is useful for drawing in large outlines on the wall and a white soluble crayon may be used to stand out against a strong background colour for finer, more detailed work.

Gliders (varnish brushes)
Made for applying varnish, soft gliders (varnish brushes) boast a fine design with no straying hairs. They stand as perfect brushes to cut in one colour up to another.

Household brushes
Large household brushes are required for preparing your wall with the necessary base coats. The smaller 2.5cm (1in) brush (above) is a little gem for mixing glazes, blocking in colour and stippling through stencil card.

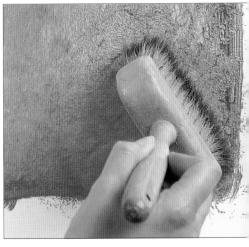

Badger softener
Acrylic glazes are beautifully softened with the tips of the badger softener. Always hold the brush perpendicular to the wall and treat it, the King of the Brushes, with great care.

Paints, glazes and varnishes

Throughout the projects, the paints, glazes and varnishes used are all water based and quick drying. Drying times vary with different temperatures and manufacturers, and labels should be read and noted. Emulsion (latex) and acrylic glazes are re-coatable on the same day. Varnishes are trickier; some only require two hours before re-coating, while others suggest six. The longer you leave varnish to dry between coats, the better. Be sure to clean your brushes thoroughly with warm water and a mild detergent at the end of each day. A wire brush is a helpful tool for this job. For brushes you are using repeatedly throughout the day, keep a paint kettle of water close to hand in which to place them between jobs. This will prevent them from hardening.

The following is a useful list of the paints, glazes and varnishes that you will need.

Matt emulsion (latex)
Available in literally thousands of different colours, this is a straightforward, chalky paint with a dead, flat finish. Widely used for standard decoration, it is recommended for use in the large blocked in areas in the demonstrated projects.

Acrylic (latex) eggshell
Tougher than matt emulsion (latex), acrylic eggshell dries with a mid-sheen finish. This paint is suitable for woodwork and can be used as a base for acrylic glazes. Due to its durability, it is the recommended base for floors when acrylic glaze is to be applied.

Vinyl silk emulsion (satin latex)
First cousin to matt emulsion (latex), this paint has a mid-sheen finish. It is used as the base coat for acrylic glazes on walls and is suitable for standard decoration in areas where walls need to be wiped frequently.

Gold and silver metallic paint
There are many shades of gold and silver metallic and these are available in liquid, tube and spray form. Many are fine imitations of real gold and silver leaf. They cover well and dry quickly.

Acrylic varnish
There is an unrecognized art to varnishing. Every part of the wall should be covered, with no areas missed or overloaded. Runs, drips and coarse brush strokes will show. Flat, satin and gloss varnishes are available, with two coats usually required. It is imperative to varnish painted floors and a more resilient floor varnish is recommended for this. Kitchens and bathrooms will benefit from the extra protection, but other areas in the home may be left unvarnished, if preferred.

Acrylic pigment
Used throughout the projects, these tubes of artist's colour may be worked in concentrated form, mixed with others, used to tint emulsion (latex) or diluted to mix acrylic glazes (see opposite). Their opacity varies. Yellow ochre, for example, should cover in one coat, whereas several coats are required for the red hues. Be guided by the Paint directory (see pages 108–113) for colour mixing.

Acrylic glaze
Diluted with water and mixed with acrylic pigments, this colourless medium is used for broken colour paint finishes such as frottage in the murals projects (see page 82) and for shadow lines and blending colours in the trompe l'oeil section.

Mixing an acrylic glaze
First, dilute the glaze with water. Different brands will require slightly varied proportions and the consistency should be aligned to milk. Two-thirds glaze to one-third water is the general proportion. Stir them together in a paint kettle and then add the acrylic pigments. Practise and experiment with colour mixing and your confidence will build.

CLEANING BRUSHES

Here, white emulsion (latex) is combed out of a household brush with a wire brush before it is thoroughly cleaned in warm water and a mild detergent.

1 In two clean glass jars measure approximately two-thirds glaze to one-third water. Pour the glaze and water into a paint kettle and stir together with a brush.

2 Slowly add acrylic pigment to create the required coloured glaze (be guided by the Paint directory, see pages 108–113) and stir once again thoroughly.

Transferring designs

As the prepared wall gleams before you in pristine anticipation, alarm bells can ring with rather a resonance. Your insurance policy is the pot of base colour paint that sits reassuringly beside you. Be sure to always save enough of this to paint out any mistakes. No line is ever absolute; with the base coat it is obliterated easily and dries in a flash.

Freehand method

The majority of mural projects in this book, and certainly all the trompe l'oeil examples, are copied from preliminary drawings directly onto the wall or ceiling. Pencil and white water-soluble crayon are used for the more detailed works, with charcoal for the bigger projects, such as the Theatrical drape (see pages 56–9). Always beat off excess charcoal with a rag or dry brush first before you add any paint.

Stencilling method

For repeated pattern and shape, as seen in the kilim motifs (see pages 26–9), the use of stencils is invaluable. Small images that require you to block in quickly before details are added, such as the seagull in Beyond the bath (see pages 38–41), can also be achieved more quickly with a stencil.

Projector method

Foolproof results can be gained by projecting your drawn image onto the wall. The further away from the wall you place the projector, the larger the image will be. Simply draw around the projected shapes with charcoal.

Tracing method

This is particularly useful for transferring a symmetrical image. With the left-hand side already drawn, it is traced. The reversed tracing can painlessly produce a mirror image to complete the right-hand side. Provided that they are not too large, other asymmetric sections of murals and trompe l'oeils may be traced onto the wall. The symmetrical hot-air balloon and its asymmetric inhabitants (see pages 14–17) were transferred with tracing paper.

1 The left-hand side of the urn was first drawn onto the wall. It was then traced. Here, the tracing paper is removed.

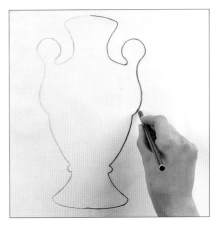

2 Now reverse the tracing and place it in position. Trace the line again to complete the right-hand mirror image.

Grid method

This steady system helps you to enlarge designs onto the wall. Your drawing must be accurate for this. Draw horizontal and vertical lines 2.5cm (1in) apart all over the drawing. With a spirit level (bubble level) and soft pencil, draw a similarly enlarged grid on the wall. To do this, multiply the size of the drawing by however many times is appropriate for the design and the size of the wall. For example, when multiplied by six, the grid squares would be 15cm (6in). Now copy your design square by square onto the wall. On completion, the redundant lines from the guiding grid are painted out with the base colour.

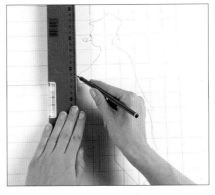

1 Horizontal and vertical lines are added over the surface area of the drawing. Here, they are spaced 2.5cm (1in) apart.

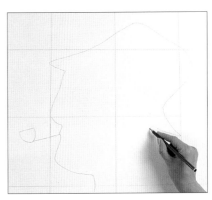

2 Draw in the enlarged grid on the wall with soft pencil and a spirit level (bubble level), then copy the contents of each square from the smaller grid to the large wall grid. This example has been enlarged six times.

DRAWING A CIRCLE

Decide on the size of circle you want and attach one end of a piece of string to the drawing pin (thumb tack) in the centre. Secure this with your thumb. Pull the string taut to the circumference. Tie a loose knot in the string at this point and push the pencil through the hole. Tighten the knot. Hold the pencil perpendicular to the wall and swing it in a confident manner until the circle is complete.

Stencilling

The method of punching paint through stencils is an ancient one and something that almost everybody can accomplish easily. To produce borders, friezes and other repeated pattern, stencilling is the obvious quick answer. You will be enthused by its speed and delighted with the effects that can be achieved.

Designs may be traced from other sources and traced again onto your stencil card. Transparent acetate may be used instead of the waxed card if it is easier to find. Cutting out the stencil with a scalpel takes a little practice and needs to be as precise as possible. A cutting mat is a good idea as it will protect your work surface and your scalpel, but it is not imperative. To achieve the best results, it is important to work in a systematic fashion. This will contribute to the smooth running of the whole job and the result will look much neater.

Stencilling can vary in character. Soft thin paint may be stippled through the waxed card to leave patchy areas in the centre of shapes. This will add a lightness and more of the three-dimensional, feminine effect that is often found in Dutch painted furniture. Solid block stencils are more direct and primitive, and they tend to be more fun.

The Kilim painted and Flower-strewn floors (see pages 26–9 and 36–7) rely heavily on the stencilling technique. Other mural projects, such as the porthole in Spaceship porthole (see pages 32–5) have used stencils to achieve certain shapes much more quickly.

> **STENCILLING TIPS**
>
> Here are some practical suggestions to help improve your stencilling:
>
> ◆ Whichever style is desired, a dry stencil brush is always required. When working with three brushes, use three dry ones.
>
> ◆ To avoid furry edges, dribbles and an untidy look, never overload your dry brush with paint and always stipple out any excess on newspaper before you begin.
>
> ◆ Keep your stencils clean and be careful not to let unwanted paint find its way onto the back of them.

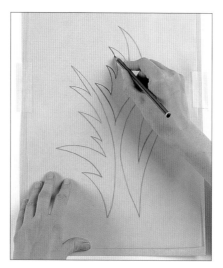

Cutting and using a stencil
1 With a sharp pencil, trace the design onto a piece of waxed stencil card. To prevent the tracing paper from slipping, secure it to the flat surface with low-tack masking tape.

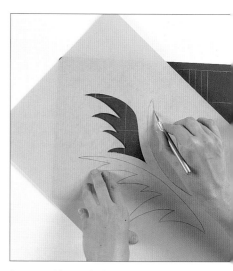

2 Now with a scalpel and a steady hand, follow the traced lines and carefully cut out the shapes. A stencil cutting mat will cushion the cutting comfortably.

3 For large stencils such as this one, spray the reverse of the stencil with an adhesive spray. This will ensure that the stencil sticks easily in position on the wall. (Use low-tack masking tape to secure smaller stencils.)

4 Stipple the paint through the cut-out stencil. To ensure a crisp edge, concentrate on covering the outside edges with precision and a dry standard household brush.

Applying paint

Here are some invaluable techniques that will help you to achieve better results with your projects.

Cutting in

This is the expression used for painting one colour faultlessly directly up to another as seen in Up, up and away (see pages 14–17) and Beyond the bath (see pages 38–41). Be sure the first colour is dry before cutting in with the next.

Blocking in

Throughout the demonstrated projects, the step photographs depict the final layer of colour being applied to the flat areas. Matt emulsion (latex) does not cover in one layer and two coats are required. Acrylic pigments vary in density. For a thin translucent effect, one coat will be sufficient but for more opaque results, two coats are probably required.

Low-tack masking tape

With this useful device, small stencils are held easily in place and straight lines can be achieved in an instant. Standard masking tape is too adhesive for such delicate jobs and will often rip off the existing paint beneath the stencil, ruining your careful work. The low-tack version of masking tape has been available for the last ten years and can be found in good decorating stores.

Cutting in
In this example, orange is cut in to white. Neatly designed and very controllable, the glider (varnish brush) is perfect for this exercise. Low-tack masking tape is little help as the two colours are invariably on a curve and the line produced would be too rigid.

Blocking in
1 Here, an orange square is in the process of being blocked in with a glider (varnish brush). Notice how the layer is quite patchy.

2 Once the first layer is dry, apply a second coat for a solid final result.

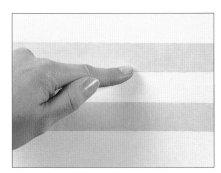

Creating perfect lines
1 Having first ruled soft pencil lines in the correct position, stick two tram lines of low-tack masking tape along each outer edge. Press the tape firmly with your fingertip to avoid any possibility of paint seeping out from under the edges as you stipple it.

2 Here, a large fitch is used to stipple in the emerald green paint. However, a 2.5cm (1in) household brush would be just as effective. Pay great attention to the extreme edges of the tape and, like stencilling, do not overload your brush with paint.

3 Now carefully peel away the masking tape on either side to reveal a perfect line of stippled paint.

Paint finishes

When painting murals, floors and trompe l'oeils, to know a little about paint finishes is a great advantage. There will often be large areas to cover and a broken colour can often be more interesting and appropriate than a flat one.

The Mock stone floor (see pages 30–1) includes sponging and frottage for the granite and stone slabs respectively. The Cave creation (see pages 20–3) also uses these techniques to achieve the textured wall. Here, these paint finishes shall be explored a little further. Skies are obvious areas that benefit from the effects of broken colour and the technique of painting a sky is covered in Up, up and away (see pages 14–17).

Acrylic glaze is the required medium for creating paint finishes. It sinks into a porous surface such as matt emulsion (latex) and needs to 'dance' on a base coat that dries to a mid-sheen. Vinyl silk emulsion (satin latex) is recommended for walls. Acrylic eggshell (latex) is recommended for floors due to its toughness.

Sponging

The natural sponge is a handy piece of equipment. Prolong its life by always washing it well in warm water and mild detergent after use. Forget the idea of using an ordinary decorator's sponge; its constitution is far too manufactured and tight for the loose abandoned effect you want. .Step 2 of Cave creation (see page 20) is an example of sponging a whole wall to increase the textured finish. Acrylic glaze is painted on the wall in areas of roughly 1 square metre (a little more than 10.5 square feet) at a time. The area is quickly sponged before the adjacent one is painted. If the whole area is painted before it is sponged, it will start to dry and become too sticky and immoveable.

Basic sponging
1 First paint the acrylic glaze on the wall with a household brush. Use a 10cm (4in) brush for large walls.

2 With a natural sponge, gently pad the wall to remove some glaze and to leave the textured imprint. Bend your wrist and change direction to produce a livelier effect.

Granite effects

The design of the Mock stone floor (see pages 30–1) is dependent on the simple green granite squares and border for its strength and purpose. In this paint finish, the imprint of the natural sponge has a fossilized appearance. It is therefore ideal for helping in the process of assimilating stone, rock and sometimes marble. Apart from sponging glaze off the surface to reveal some of the background colour, a deeper shade can be sponged on as a second layer to intensify the depth of colour (see step 4 below). Take the granite a stage further and it assumes the character of porphyry (see step 5). Dots of colour are spattered over the dried surface. When spattering, there is often a tendency to go wild. Restrain yourself and avoid overloading your brush. For a small decorative diamond, fine specks rather than splodges are preferable.

Simple granite
1 The diamond was first measured on crossed pencil lines. Low-tack masking tape was applied to the outer edges and here, red vinyl silk emulsion (satin latex) is blocked in with a glider (varnish brush).

2 Paint a coat of dark red acrylic glaze over the emulsioned surface.

3 Sponge the glaze with a natural sponge. Leave to dry.

4 First dip the sponge in an umber glaze and then pat softly over some areas to increase the depth of colour.

5 Dip a small household brush in cream acrylic. Flick small dots over the surface of the diamond to give the granite a rather superior porphyry character.

Frottage

This simple device, dignified by the name of frottage, has frequently been used to obtain textured effects in abstract painting. To produce the image of a coin by rubbing over a thin piece of paper is perhaps the simplest form of frottage. To 'rub' is to frottage.

When applied to acrylic glaze, the frottage technique is riveting and absurdly easy. If you are executing a whole wall, the glaze should be painted in areas of roughly 1 square metre (a little more than 10.5 square feet) and frottaged immediately while the glaze is workably wet. Quickly return to your household brush and lay on the next section, working across and down the wall alternately.

As the cheapest alternative, newspaper is used throughout all the frottage examples in this book. Brown paper and wrapping paper are other options and they avoid the possible hazard of newsprint being transferred to the wall. However, if you work quickly, then the newspaper hiccup can be avoided. In contrast to the subdued Mock stone floor frottage (see pages 30–1) and the earth colours of the Cave creation (see pages 20–3), a swimming pool blue is demonstrated here and built up with two layers of frottage.

Creating frottage
1 With a household brush, paint the acrylic glaze on the wall. Here, there is no need for absolute consistency.

2 Lay a sheet of newspaper over the glazed surface. With a bunched muslin rag, gently rub it over the surface to ensure connection with the wall.

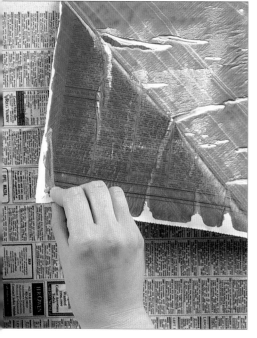

3 Peel the paper away from the wall as quickly as possible. If you leave it too long, unwanted newsprint is your added extra.

4 Once the first frottage of glaze is dry, repeat the procedure by painting the second layer of glaze (above). As soon as the newspaper has been gently rubbed with a muslin rag as before, peel back the paper (opposite) to reveal a gloriously rich layer of double frottage.

Painting stone

Stone is a natural substance with infinite varieties of texture and pattern. To achieve a convincing effect, you have to aim for a random nature and yet still be aware of the consistent patterns within different stones. Whenever you can, pick up pieces of rock and pebbles, polished or rough, and just look at the minute patterns and myriad colours. Reliable techniques include stippling, sponging and spattering (see pages 78. 80 and 81). A mixture of all three can be used when creating stone. Build up a series of glazes over the base colour to get increasingly complex textures. As ever, practice throws up all sorts of wonderful accidents to be played upon. The pressure, heat and erosion that affects a stone over thousands of years can be imitated with a few strokes of the brush and a confident approach.

Here, a cracked stone slab is prepared with pale neutral vinyl silk emulsion satin (latex).

Creating stone
1 Mix a thin acrylic glaze with yellow ochre and raw umber. Paint it loosely so that it is thick in some places and faint in others. With a dusting brush, stipple the surface to soften the brush strokes and even out the glaze.

2 Put some raw and burnt umber on a palette and apply this sparingly to random areas while the first coat is still wet. With a stiff 2.5cm (1in) household brush, stipple in the darker colour, softening it here and there with the duster brush. Leave to dry.

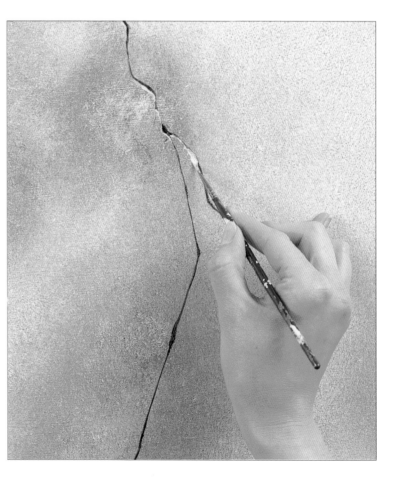

3 Use a fine artist's brush (above) to create cracks in the stone. Drag some of the burnt umber in raggedy lines across the stone, varying the thickness as you go. Mix the highlight colour with the acrylic glaze and some white. Paint one side of the crack, again varying its thickness against the dark line (opposite). This will accentuate the craggy character of the stone.

Painting fabric

Whether a light linen or swathes of heavy velvet, the painting of fabric appears to be a daunting task, but it can be broken down into easy steps. Be patient and don't be disheartened during the early stages when you wonder how on earth the image will ever pull together.

As previously mentioned in the Theatrical drape project (see pages 56–9), there is simply no substitute for looking at the real thing and practising with pencil and paper before you begin. This is time pricelessly spent. Unlike the Theatrical drape, where the stripes do a lot of the convincing for you, this exercise is a painting of an unpatterned swathe of fabric. The forms and folds of the material are rendered solely in tones of light and shade. First, prepare the background with a white matt emulsion (latex). Now draw the outline of the shapes in pencil; be free with the sweeping movement of the gentle curves of the fabric, the sudden breaks and their irregular widths.

Depicting fabric
1 When you are satisfied with the shape of the falling fabric, paint the yellow background colour with a household brush. Then mix an acrylic shadow glaze with burnt sienna. Using a medium-sized fitch, paint in the shadows in the crevices and folds.

2 With some white, paint the highlight to the tops of the folds. Vary the width of the brush strokes depending on the size of the fold.

3 Finally, with a slightly diluted acrylic shadow glaze, expand the original shadow lines and accentuate the depth and three-dimensional quality of the drapery.

Painting shadow and highlights

The shadow is an essential weapon in your armoury, along with its counterpart, the highlight. Shadows are the essence of what locates the depicted object in space. Whenever you are about to paint something on the wall, place a real object against it and look to see in which direction the real shadow falls; also note its density. Allow reality to be your cue: it is, after all, what you are trying to achieve.

Shiny objects have a striking highlight. The rougher the surface becomes, the more diffused its highlight appears. Think of the difference between the shine on a freshly peeled boiled egg and the sheen on an eggshell, or the stark highlight on satin when compared to the soft light on denim.

When choosing your subject, take some time to study the real thing. Observe how and where the light falls upon it. In the example that follows, you will see that a shiny blue ball is almost white where it reflects the light and nearly black when it is in deep shadow. It isn't just blue: it is a black, dark blue, mid-blue, light blue and white; a disc of many colours. The shadow beneath it is the last step that transforms it into a real ball or sphere.

The exercise on this page demonstrates in simple stages how the light and shade create depth and weight.

Blue sphere
1 Draw a circle with a compass and paint it blue with a fitch or small glider (varnish brush). Squeeze some blue, Payne's grey and white onto a palette. Mix the grey and blue together and paint the bottom left sector.

2 With some of the base blue, gently soften the edge of the shadow into the main body of the circle.

3 Mix some blue and white together and paint the top right part of the circle.

4 Working quickly, apply the base blue to the centre of the circle and soften into the two other colours. Work the colours into each other until there is a smooth transition between them.

5 When the paint is dry, add a stark white highlight to the top right of the circle. Follow the curve of the outer edge (above). With Payne's grey, add an elliptical shadow below and to the right of the circle (opposite).

INSPIRATIONS

The following pages feature some exquisite examples of murals and trompe l'oeil. The majority were commissioned by private clients, while others have been painted in the home of the artist. Some are large in scale and grand in subject matter, but others are more discreet and hold a jokey element. All are impressive, striking works of art. They have been selected to inspire and delight you, and to show you how, with a little time and practice, great things can be produced.

The fine example of trompe l'oeil (above) was painted by Ian Cairnie. On a table's surface awaits 'bad news' ... the final demand of a gas bill, a memo from a car mechanic claiming a new clutch is needed in the car and a torn-off button from an item of clothing. Perhaps worst of all, on the tabletop also lies a postcard from a friend in Italy who says they are having a wonderful time, that they are in love and that everything is 'perfect'! The realism of this piece is almost daunting.

Opposite: Charlotte Wright has created a crumbling Italian atmosphere in the basement of her home. With no natural light available, she decided to paint wooden floorboards on part of the ceiling, with strips of sky peeping through. Strands of painted ivy weave their way in from the outside world, adding a natural element.

Above left: In this detail taken from the swimming pool (below left), a female nude gently reclines among a flowing drape and a collection of seashells. The classical trompe l'oeil introduces a feeling of great serenity and cleverly fills a lunette at one end of the swimming pool.

Striking grandeur and a new dimension is added to a swimming pool in Canada (left) by the painted sky above and sun drenched panorama at one end. This was a private commission by Charlotte Wright and Sarah Hocombe of Angel Interiors.

Right: Painted in the curved corner of a dining room painted by Simon Brady, this ruined colonnade invites you to miraculously walk into the Italian landscape.

This collection of seven French plates hanging on a wall (left) was painted by Charlotte Wright as a private commission. The trompe l'oeil plates with their contrasting shapes and pattern were painted off site and then stuck to the wall afterwards. Shadows were added in once the plates were in their final position.

The grand scale and glorious subject matter of the mural below are extremely impressive. It adorns a large wall in the Mount Nelson Hotel in Cape Town. Painted by Simon Brady, the mural is set in 1860. The rich foreground, although historically correct, has actually been taken from the artist's imagination. Beyond, the landscape is painted from life and shows a view of the back of Table Mountain.

Right: Here, the deep shadow, bright highlights and receding perspective of the tiled floor create a very convincing illusion of space. Simon Brady was commissioned by the owner of this board to paint these fine examples of Chinese porcelain using the original sketches that his grandfather made when he added to the collection. The sketchbooks are all that remain of the collection.

Below: The
complete mural.

This design for a 75 metre (246 feet) super
yacht was conceived by Donald Starkey
Designs. The continuous mural, stretching
roughly 12 metres (39 feet) vertically through
four decks, was painted by dkt Specialist
Decoration. When viewed from the glass
walled elevator, you can travel the depths of
the ocean to the hazy brilliance of a tropical
beach. This is a unique and inspired concept.

Below, left and opposite: Detailed sections of
the vibrant mural.

Below: Painted by Roderick Booth-Jones, this is a fine example of a stone niche with a hedonistic air. The shelves are full of luxurious items, such as a classic car, sliced avocados and wine. These are all things that the private commissioner particularly enjoys and together they form a unique trompe l'oeil that is utterly personal.

This trompe l'oeil of a niche (above) was painted on board and is designed to be hung at eye level. Created by Simon Brady, it was a private commission. The two shelves are full of special things that are personal to the family: photographs of various members, a globe to signify their travels, pertinent books, five scrabble tiles with a cryptic message, and so on.

The display cabinet (opposite) was commissioned by London based interior designer Suzanne Marks. It was painted by Angel Interiors and is personalized with charming elements such as an old wedding invitation belonging to the owners. The various book titles were chosen by the family for sentimental reasons. An open bottle of champagne stands on the fourth shelf down and quirky details, such as the abandoned artists brushes, are typical of the humour often employed in trompe l'oeil painting. The piece is signed by way of a book, itself entitled *Trompe L'oeil Painting* by Charlotte Wright.

The subtle colours and shading of the firescreen below, painted by Simon Brady, sit well in a plain white marble fireplace. It is an old idea to cover the fireplace in the summer months with a board to hide the blackened grate.

Right: Here, you see almost two thirds of a magnificent ceiling painted by Tim Salandin, Roger Byrne and Mark Callup. A private commission for a dining room, the brief given by the designer to Tim was 'Mythology as related to astrology'. The central zodiacal panel is surrounded by eight separate scenes of beautiful gods and goddesses. Verte Antique and Sicilian are just two of the eleven different types of marble that have been superbly painted to strengthen and complement the compositions within the various panels.

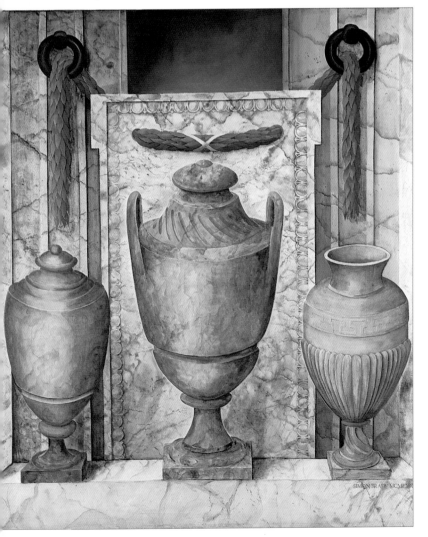

Bruce Church was asked by his clients to paint a ceiling inspired by the Italian Renaissance. On a backdrop of soft blue sky, six delightful cherubs, one holding a dove and another a basket of purple flowers, overlook a curved balustrade. A parakeet perched on a berried branch adds a touch of effective strong colour to the ceiling.

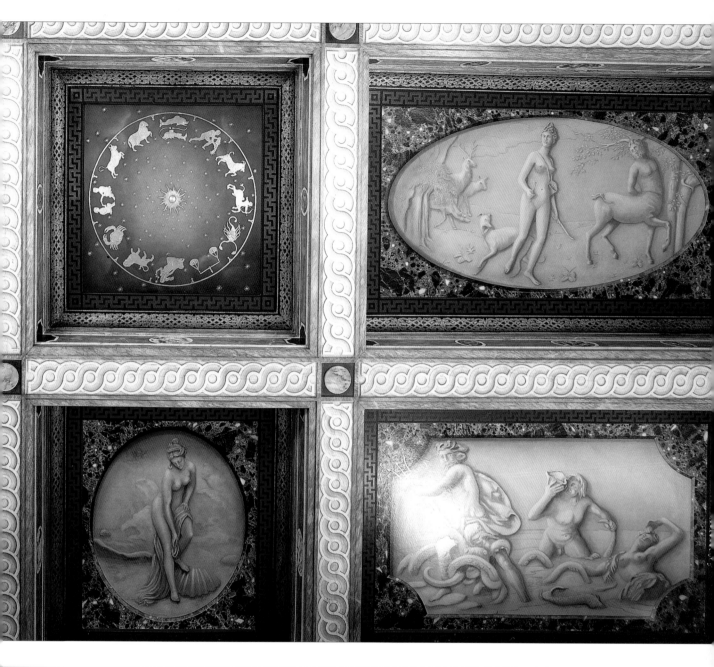

Ideally suited to a child's bedroom, this simple mural of animals queuing up to board the ark is a decorative scene. Painted by Victoria Ellerton, the strong colours and easily recognizable animals create an appealing backdrop for children to play against.

Left: Here, heavy theatrical draperies are a clever way of disguising the hard angle caused by the staircase. Based on the 17th-century 'Commedia del Arte', the central harlequin was one of the main characters in the travelling theatrical group. This flamboyant mural and its architectural panels beneath were painted as a private commission by Bruce Church.

Shutters are cleverly incorporated into 'A Peep into the Big Top' (below). The curtain is held back by a seated clown. Painted by Roderick Booth-Jones, the vibrant colours and flying acrobats give the circus a strong sense of excitement and fun.

The geometric wall painting (above) is to be found in a corridor at the Palazzo Davanzati in Florence. Painted at the end of the 14th century, its classic pattern is quite timeless. The soft greens and terra-cotta red have weathered the test of time beautifully.

In the centre of
Florence at Palazzo
Davanzati, some of
the finest examples
of richly painted
wall decorations are
to be found. This
medieval house,
built at the end of
the 14th century,
and its painted
allegories, myths
and geometric
designs, is a feast
for the eyes. A
section from the
Parakeet room (left)
shows a combina-
tion of architectural
trompe l'oeil and
botanical pattern.

Inspired by the Casbah, Simon Brady
has produced an exotic and mysterious
suggestion of things going on behind the
North African wooden screen (below). Spices
and herbs hang from the wall and the
beautiful carpet hangs casually out of the
window.

Right: Based on murals in the Palazzo
Davanzati in Florence, Simon Brady took the
tree of life motif and used stencils and other
techniques to create a richly coloured frieze
around the top of a panelled drawing room.

Beautifully painted by Bruce Church, the female flautist (below) stands within a niche and is inspired by a Viennese palace. Executed on an outside brick wall, the niche is surrounded by panels of painted Renaissance carvings, all of which result in a muted and highly successful trompe l'oeil.

Right: This mural holds a double deception. Cleverly painted by Owen Turville on an exterior wall, it stands a metre beyond the real window and its interior blind, through which it can be seen. Painted outside a city dining room, with the gazebo in the background and dogs strolling across newly mown grass in the foreground, it reminds the clients of the peace and quiet of their country garden.

Aptly positioned in an 18th-century walled kitchen garden, this fine trompe l'oil, inspired by a painting by Arcimboldo, is painted by Owen Turville. Various techniques have been used to achieve the weathered grey stone which gives a sculptural illusion. The bust is composed of stone vegetables. A panel of carved garden tools lies beneath, with young oak trees and their roots surrounding the arched composition.

Paint directory

With the exception of pure white glazes and paints, all the colour swatches that have been used in the 18 demonstrated projects are listed below. The matt emulsion (latex) colour descriptions are more general, while the acrylic pigments are specific. Each project lists them in the order in which they were applied.

UP, UP AND AWAY (see pages 14–17)

Sky blue vinyl silk emulsion (latex): Preparation of wall.

Pale yellow matt emulsion (latex): Block in for balloon.

Stronger yellow matt emulsion (latex): Block in for stripes.

Red matt emulsion (latex): Swags, diamonds and handkerchief.

White, raw umber: Texture and definition on basket.

Dark blue purple matt emulsion (latex): Sandbags and telescope.

Black matt emulsion (latex): Figures and anchor.

White, Payne's grey: Balloon strings.

NOCTURNAL CITY SKYLINE
(see pages 18–19)

Deep blue matt emulsion (latex): Preparation of upper section of wall.

Black matt emulsion (latex): Preparation of lower section of wall.

White, Naples yellow: Windows.

Metallic acrylic gold: Moon and stars.

CAVE CREATION (see pages 20–3)

Off-white vinyl silk emulsion (latex): Preparation of wall.

Yellow ochre, raw umber acrylic glaze: For frottage.

Burnt sienna acrylic glaze: For sponging.

Burnt umber, ivory black: Bison outlines.

Burnt sienna, burnt umber: Cracks.

Burnt sienna: Fingertips and hand print.

Raw umber acrylic glaze: Final ageing layer.

SIMPLE SILHOUETTES (see pages 24–5)

Cream matt emulsion (latex): Preparation of wall.

Black matt emulsion (latex): Block in for figures.

KILIM PAINTED FLOOR (see pages 26–9)

Terracotta matt emulsion (latex): Preparation of wooden floor, diamond stencils.

Pale orange matt emulsion (latex): Horizontal wide stripes.

Black matt emulsion (latex): Border.

Ultramarine blue: Horizontal thin stripes.

Warm cream matt emulsion (latex): Lozenge shapes, smaller stencils.

Prussian blue matt emulsion (latex): Stencils.

Hooker's green, ivory black: Stencils.

MOCK STONE FLOOR (see pages 30–1)

Cream acrylic (latex) eggshell: Preparation of wooden floor-boards.

Yellow ochre, raw umber acrylic glaze: For frottage.

Stone matt emulsion (latex): Grouting lines.

Green acrylic latex eggshell: Granite base colour.

Hooker's green, ivory black acrylic glaze: For sponging granite.

SPACESHIP PORTHOLE (see pages 32–5)

Strong yellow matt emulsion (latex): Preparation of wall.

Cadmium orange: Diagonal stripes.

Black emulsion (latex): Block in for porthole.

Metallic acrylic silver: Block in for porthole frame, stars and planet. Aerosol spray used for rocket.

Cadmium red: Porthole bolts and detailing on rocket.

Metallic acrylic silver, ivory black: Porthole outer rim.

FLOWER-STREWN FLOOR (see pages 36–7)

Soft green matt emulsion (latex): Preparation of floor-boards. Highlights on berries.

Hooker's green: Largest stencil.

White, Hooker's green: Tulip stalk and leaves.

White, Naples yellow: Tulip head.

Crimson lake, cadmium red: Berries.

White, Naples yellow, yellow ochre: Detail on tulip head.

BEYOND THE BATH (see pages 38–41)

Sky blue matt emulsion (latex): Block in for sky.

Deep blue matt emulsion (latex): Block in for sea.

White, raw umber: Block in for post.

Cadmium red: Stripes for lifebelt.

White, raw umber: Woodgrain markings on post.

Raw umber: Hook.

White, yellow ochre, cadmium yellow: Block in for rope.

White, yellow ochre, raw umber: Detailing on post.

Cadmium red, cadmium orange: Bird's beak and feet.

White, Payne's grey: Detailing on seagull.

White, cadmium yellow: Foreground, sails and masts.

White, phthalo blue: Boat.

Cadmium yellow, cadmium red: Horizon boats, sails and masts.

OUTSIDE-IN (see pages 42–3)

Black matt emulsion (latex): Preparation of wall. Outlines for light and room shapes and block in for pencils, radio and crossbars.

Strong orange matt emulsion (latex): Block in for window.

White, Naples yellow: Block in for area within light.

Ultramarine blue: Block in for light.

FRAGMENT OF MASONRY (see pages 48–9)

Stone vinyl silk emulsion (satin latex): Preparation of board, highlights on cracks.

Raw umber thin acrylic glaze: Texture.

Raw umber: Addition to texture, cracks.

Raw umber thicker glaze: Hard shadow around dentils.

Stone vinyl silk emulsion (satin latex), raw umber, Payne's grey: Shadow glaze.

HANG IT ALL (see pages 50–3)

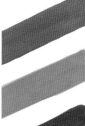

Deep red matt emulsion (latex): Preparation of wall

Yellow ochre: Block in for brass elements.

Burnt umber: Block in for dog lead.

White, Payne's grey: Block in for catapult.

Burnt sienna: Shadow on brass elements.

White, yellow ochre: Highlights on brass elements.

White, raw sienna: Edge of dog lead.

Payne's grey: Shadow of catapult.

Payne's grey, burnt umber: Sling of catapult.

Burnt umber acrylic glaze: Shadows on wall.

PLATE IN A GRATE (see pages 54–5)

Mid-grey matt emulsion (latex): Preparation of board.

White, Payne's grey: Shadows within grate.

Increased white, Payne's grey: Plate's shadow.

White, phthalo blue, lemon yellow: Block in for plate.

Phthalo blue: Borders and decorative detail on plate.

Chromium oxide green: Leaf design on plate.

Payne's grey acrylic glaze: Shadow on plate.

THEATRICAL DRAPE (see pages 56–9)

Warm sand matt emulsion (latex): Preparation of wall.

Deeper sand acrylic (latex) eggshell: Skirting board (baseboard).

Yellow ochre: Block in for brass rail and boss.

Burnt sienna: Shadow on brass elements.

White, yellow ochre: Highlights on brass elements.

Off-white matt emulsion (latex): Block in for curtain.

Burnt sienna matt emulsion (latex): Stripes on curtain.

Payne's grey thin acrylic glaze: Shadow leading up to folds.

Increased Payne's grey in acrylic glaze: Shadow closer to the line of folds.

RED HOT CHILLI PEPPERS (see pages 60–1)

Off-white matt emulsion (latex): Preparation of wall.

Acra red: Block in for chillis.

White, yellow ochre, raw umber: Block in for string and stalks.

Cadmium red, burnt umber: Definition on chillis.

Cadmium red, increased burnt umber: Detailing on string and stalks.

Payne's grey acrylic glaze: Shadows.

ROSE TRELLIS ARCH (see pages 62–65)

Soft cream matt emulsion (latex): Preparation of wall.

White, ultramarine: Sky beneath arch.

White, light permanent green: Block in for hedge.

Light permanent green: Hedge texture.

White and raw umber diluted with water: Block in forflagstones, shadow to left of fountain on flagstones.

White, raw umber: Left side of arch, fountain highlights.

Raw umber: Cracks between flagstones.

White, burnt umber (the amount of white and therefore the depth of colour varies between the three areas): Wall, right side of arch, stems of roses.

Sap green: Leaves, plants and shrubs; tufts of grass.

White, cadmium red: Block in for rose flowerheads.

White, increased cadmium red: Petal shadows.

A little white and raw umber: Block in for fountain.

GOTHIC CUBES (see pages 66–7)

Sand matt emulsion (latex): Preparation of wall. Left hand plane of cubes.

Strong blue matt emulsion (latex): Block in for cubes.

Dark red acrylic (latex) eggshell: Skirting board (baseboard) and door.

FLY THE FLAGS (see pages 68–71)

Soft cream matt emulsion (latex): Preparation of wall.

Yellow ochre: Flagpoles.

Cadmium red: Block in for base colour of flag, ribbon.

Ultramarine blue: Block in for base colour of flags.

Cadmium yellow: Block in for base colour of flag, ribbon.

Payne's grey acrylic glaze: Shadow beside fold.

White, ultramarine blue: Highlight to edge of fold.

White, cadmium yellow: Highlight to edge of fold.

White, cadmium red: Highlight on back of fold.

Burnt umber, yellow ochre: Shadow on poles.

White, yellow ochre: Highlight on poles.

White, burnt umber acrylic glaze: Shadow beneath flags and beside ribbons.

Templates

On the following pages you will find templates for the majority of the stencils used in the mural and floor projects. Note that they are not actual size. Patterns for the balloon, Rome skyline, and bison are also included and these may be copied, traced or enlarged on a photocopier. To decorate your own floors or walls, trace and transfer the designs to stencil card (see page 78) and enlarge them to suit your design. Natural history books, decorative wrapping paper and magazines are just a few of the many other places where you will find further sources to trace and stencil.

KILIM PAINTED FLOOR
(see pages 26–9)

FLOWER-STREWN FLOOR
(See pages 36–7)

NOCTURNAL CITY SKYLINE
(See pages 18–19)

SPACESHIP PORTHOLE
(See pages 32–5)

SIMPLE SILHOUETTES
(See pages 24–5)

BEYOND THE BATH
(See pages 38–41)

UP, UP AND AWAY
(See pages 14–17)

BASKET WEAVE STENCIL

CAVE CREATION
(See pages 20–3)

Safety

Compared with oil, water-based paints and varnishes pose fewer problems when it comes to harmful fumes. Remember that some pigments are poisonous and these can be hazardous. Do not eat, drink, smoke or rub your skin or eyes whilst you are working and always wash your hands thoroughly when you finish work. Manufacturers will often supply their own safety suggestions on labels. Pay attention to their advice. At the end of the day, it all comes down to commonsense.

Water-based paints are considerably more odourless, but it is still important to work in a well ventilated area. Masks are advisable for sensitive lungs. Plastic goggles are also available, but these should not be necessary when you are working solely with water-based paints. Both masks and goggles are recommended when sanding floors. Remember to replace lids on tins and tops on tubes. They attract stray children like magnets and should be left out of reach or tidied away. Any ladders used should be robust and placed on their side when not in use for similar reasons.

Care should be taken with scalpels, particularly when changing blades. Always dispose of blades carefully. Beware of the wire brush when cleaning your brushes. Untold damage can be done if one of the wires slips up your finger nail.

An uncluttered head and an organized approach are big advantages for planning and safety. With a drawing perfected on paper and the target well established, remove all furniture and clear as much space as possible around it. Put dust sheets (dropcloths) down on the floor.

At the end of the day, once your brushes are clean, remove all rubbish, rags and paint kettles of dirty water. Dispose of these responsibly. This is a good habit to get into and it will add a skip to your brush stroke the next morning.

Glossary

ACRYLIC LATEX EGGSHELL: Water-based paint with a mid-sheen finish. Suitable for woodwork and recommended as the base coat for acrylic glaze on floors.

ACRYLIC GLAZE: Water-based translucent medium to which acrylic pigment is added to achieve broken colour effects.

ACRYLIC PIGMENT: Water-based pure pigment.

ADHESIVE SPRAY: Aerosol fixative for holding stencils in place on the wall.

BADGER SOFTENER: Fine-quality brush made from badger hair. Used for softening broken colour acrylic glazes.

BLOCKING IN: The process of building up layers of a colour to fill an area.

BOSS: An ornamental knob or stud.

CHARCOAL: Porous black stick of partially burnt wood, sometimes used for sketching outlines of a design onto a wall or ceiling.

COMPASS: Instrument used with a pencil for drawing small circles.

CUTTING IN: The process of striking a clean line of one colour up to another.

DENTIL: Small block used in rows resembling teeth in the cornices of Classical architecture.

DISTRESSING: The technique that ages painted surfaces.

DUSTING BRUSH: Versatile hog's hair brush. A good substitute for the badger softener.

FABRIC PAINT: Used for painting or stencilling on fabrics such as blinds or curtains.

FILLER (SPACKLE): Substance used to fill holes and cracks when preparing walls.

FITCH: Long-handled hardy brush with either round or square ends.

FROTTAGE: The process of gently rubbing paper onto wet glaze and removing it to reveal an organic, asymmetric pattern.

GLIDER (VARNISH BRUSH): Fine-quality bristle brush for varnishing, but useful for delicate work such as cutting in, due to its lack of straying hairs.

GRANITE: Crystalline rock.

GROUTING LINES: Lines composed of coarse plaster used between tiles, stone, etc.

HIGHLIGHT: The part that receives maximum light.

MATT EMULSION (LATEX): Water-based paint with a dead flat, chalky finish. Suitable for walls and ceilings, and used for the larger expanses of flat colour required in murals and trompe l'oeil.

MDF: Medium density fibre. Used as a substitute for wood or chipboard.

MOULDING: Ornamental grooving or projection above or below a plane surface.

PAINT KETTLE: Small circular container with handle to hold paint, glaze or varnish.

PLUMB LINE: Heavy mass hung on a string to show the vertical line.

PORPHYRY: Speckled granite rock.

PVA: Poly vinyl adhesive.

SANDPAPER: Abrasive paper used to sand down surfaces when preparing them for paint.

STEEL WOOL: An abrasive material used for ageing painted surfaces.

STENCILLING: Technique to transfer shape or pattern onto the wall.

STIPPLING: Part of the stencilling technique, where the paint is punched through the cut-out stencil. Also used as a traditional paint finish.

VARNISH: Protective water-based resin. Available in matt, satin and gloss.

VINYL SILK EMULSION (SATIN LATEX): Water-based paint with a mid-sheen. The base required for acrylic glazes.

WIRE BRUSH: A brush that is specially designed for cleaning brushes.

Useful addresses

The following is a list of specialist decorating shops.

United Kingdom:

J.W. BOLLOM & COMPANY LIMITED
121 South Liberty Lane
Ashton Vale
Bristol BS3 2SZ
Telephone: 0117 966 5151
Fax: 0117 966 7180

C. BREWER & SONS LIMITED
327 Putney Bridge Road
London SW15 2PG
Telephone: 0181 788 9335

CRAIG & ROSE PLC
172 Leith Walk
Edinburgh EH6 5EB
Telephone: 0131 554 1131

CROWN PAINTS
P.O. Box 37
Crown House
Hollins Road
Darwen
Lancs. BB3 2BG
Telephone: 01254 704951

DULUX DECORATOR CENTRE
Clanville Road
Cowley
Oxford OX4 2DB
Telephone: 01865 374011
Fax: 01865 378343

FARROW & BALL
Uddens Trading Estate
Wimborne
Dorset BHY21 7NL
Telephone: 01202 876141

GREEN & STONE
259 Kings Road
London SW3
Telephone: 0171 352 0837

JOHN OLIVER PAINTS
33 Pembridge Road
London W11 3HG
Telephone: 0171 221 6466

LEYLAND SDM (branches all over London)
361–65 Kensington High Street
London W14 8QY
Freephone: 0800 454 484
E mail: advert@Leyland SDM.co.uk

NUTSHELL NATURAL PAINT
Hamlyn House
Mardle Way
Buckfastleigh
Devon TQ11 ONR
Telephone: 0136 464 2892
Fax: 01364 643 888

THE PAINT SERVICE COMPANY
19 Eccleston Street
London SW1 9LX

PAPERS AND PAINTS LIMITED
4 Park Walk
London SW10 0AD
Telephone: 0171 352 8626
Fax: 0171 352 1017
E mail: sales@papers-paints.co.uk

POTMOLEN PAINTS
27 Woodcock Industrial Estate
Warminster
Wilts. BA12 9DX
Telephone: 01985 213960

J.H. RATCLIFFE & COMPANY
135a Linaker Street
Southport PR8 5DF
Telephone: 01704 537 999
Fax: 01704 544138

SIMPSONS PAINTS LIMITED
122–124 Broadley Street
London NW5 8BB
Telephone: 0171 723 3762

USA:

General craft and paint supplies

HOBBY LOBBY
7707 SW 44th Street
Oklahoma City, OK 73179
Tel: (405) 745-1100
Web site: http://www.hobbylobby.com

HOME DEPOT U.S.A., Inc.
2455 Paces Ferry Road
Atlanta, GA 30339-4024
Tel: (770) 433-8211
Web site: http://www.homedepot.com

MICHAELS' ARTS AND CRAFTS
8000 Bent Branch Drive
Irving, TX 75063
Tel: (214) 409-1300
Web site: http://www.michaels.com

PEARL PAINT
308 Canal Street
New York, NY 10013
Tel: (212) 431-7932
Web site: http://www.pearlpaint.com

BRUSHES AND PAINTS
Back Street, Inc.
3905 Steve Reynolds Blvd.
Norcross, GA 30093
Tel: (770) 381-7373
Fax: (770) 381-6424

Glazes, glues and varnishes:

CRAFTCO INDUSTRIES, INC.
410 Wentworth Street North
Hamilton, Ontario, Canada L8L 5W3
Tel: (800) 661-0010
Web site: http://www.craftco.com

DECOART
P.O. Box 386
Stanford, KY 40484
Tel: (606) 365-3193
Web site: http://www.decoart.com

DELTA TECHNICAL COATINGS
2550 Pellissier Place
Whittier, CA 90601
Tel: (800) 423-4135

SILVER BRUSH LIMITED
92 Main Street, Bldg. 18C
Windsor, NJ 08561
Tel: (609) 443-4900
Fax: (609) 443-4888

STENCILER'S EMPORIUM, INC.
1325 Armstrong Road, Suite 170
Northfield, MN 55057
Tel: (800) 229-1760

Australia:

HORNSBY PAINT WAREHOUSE
89 Hunter Street
Hornsby
NSW 2077
Australia
Telephone: 02 9477 7122

JANET'S ART SUPPLIES
143–5 Victoria Avenue
Chatswood
NSW 2067
Australia
Telephone: 02 9417 8572

Further reading

Cass, Caroline, *Grand Illusions: Contemporary Interior Murals*. Phaidon Press Ltd., 1988.
McCloud, Kevin, *Kevin McCloud's Decorating Handbook*. Dorling Kindersley, 1990.
Milman, Miriam, *Trompe L'oeil Painting: Illusions of Reality*. Macmillan London Ltd., 1982.
Rust, Graham, *The Painted House*. Macmillan London Ltd., 1988.
Seligman, Patricia, *Painting Murals*. Macdonald & Co., 1987.

Index

Authors' acknowledgements

Our underlined thanks goes to Jane Forster for her vibrant and colourful ideas, to Ed Allwright for his energy and acrobatic skills with the camera and to his assistants, Ian and Alex. To Terry Evans for the template illustrations. Also to Jane Donovan who so astutely and modestly steered the ship, and for the use of her beautiful hands in the techniques section, and to Kate Kirby at Collins & Brown for her precision and her brilliant enthusiasm, and Loryn Birkholtz also at Collins & Brown, who has been a great help.

Victoria Ellerton wishes to pass on her special thanks to the following people. To Sarah Cox for giving up her walls for a week. To Rose Chisholm, Jane Garton, Toby Nuttall, Kate Bologna, Kay MacCauley and Joanna Belton for their professional advice; her family, friends and godchildren for their patience and understanding during this absurdly busy spate. To Nicola Wood for modelling in the original presentation. And lastly, to Simon for jumping aboard to become her counterpart, giving the trompe l'oeil section life and for making her laugh till she cried.

Publisher's acknowledgements

Collins & Brown and Jane Forster would like to thank the following individuals and companies who kindly supplied props for photography:

BEYOND THE BATH (see pages 38–41) Bathroom accessories: Natural Facts Ltd, 192 Kings Road, Chelsea SW3 5XP (0171 352 4283)

CAVE CREATION (see pages 20–3) Boxes: The Holding Company, 243–245 Kings Road, London SW3 5EL (0171 532 1600).

THEATRICAL DRAPE (see pages 56–9) Chair: Nordic Style, 109 Lots Road, London SW10 0RN (0171 351 1755).

FLOWER-STREWN FLOOR (see pages 36–7) Cushion: The Pier, 200 Tottenham Court Road, London W1P 0AD (0171 637 7001).

KILIM PAINTED FLOOR (see pages 26–9) Ceramic bowl: Sarah Willis Ceramics, 10 Picton Place, Narberth, Pembrokeshire SA24 7BE (01834 860626). Ceramic pot: Neal Street East, 5 Neal Street, London WC2H 9PU (0171 240 0135) Curtain: The Pier, 200 Tottenham Court Road, London W1P 0AD (0171 637 7001) Tiles: Worlds End Tiles, Silverthorne Road, Battersea, London SW8 3HE (0171 819 2100)

NOCTURNAL CITY SKYLINE (see pages 18–19) Tablecloth, glasses and cloth: The Pier, 200 Tottenham Court Road, London W1P 0AD (0171 637 7001) Chandelier and candlestick: Angelic, Highgate Business Centre, Greenwood Place, London NW5 1LB (0171 267 9299)

PLATE IN A GRATE (see pages 54–5) Ceramic bowls: Sarah Willis Ceramics, 10 Picton Place, Narberth, Pembrokeshire SA24 7BE (01834 860626) Urns: Amphora, 155 Goldhawk Road, London W12 8EN (0181 749 2320).

SIMPLE SILHOUETTES (see pages 24–5) Vases and cushion: Neal Street East, 5 Neal Street, London WC2H 9PU (0171 240 0135).

MOCK STONE FLOOR (see pages 30–1) Curtain: The Pier, 200 Tottenham Court Road, London W1P 0AD (0171 637 7001). Urns: Amphora, 155 Goldhawk Road, London W12 8EN (0181 749 2320).

Picture credits

Special thanks to the following: p8 (centre) *World of Interiors* magazine, Nicolette Le Pelley/photographer: Fritz von der Schulenburg; pp86/7 Simon Brady p88 Ian Cairnie; p89 Charlotte Wright, Angel Interiors; p90 (top and below) Charlotte Wright, Angel Interiors; p91 Simon Brady p92 Charlotte Wright, Angel Interiors; p93 (top) Simon Brady p93 (below) The mural from the dining room at the Mount Nelson Hotel, Cape Town is by kind permission of Orient-Express Hotels; pp94/5 mural created by dkt Specialist Decoration, 3 Charterhouse Works, Eltringham Street, London SW18 1TD (44) 0181 874 3565; p96 (left) Roderick Booth-Jones p96 (right) Simon Brady p97 Charlotte Wright, Angel Interiors; p98 (left) Simon Brady pp98/9 Tim Salandin p99 (below) Bruce Church p100 (top) Victoria Ellerton/Geoff Dann p100 (below) Bruce Church; p101 Roderick Booth-Jones pp102/3 *World of Interiors* magazine, Nicolette Le Pelley/photographer: Fritz von der Schulenburg; p104/5 Simon Brady p106 (left) Bruce Church pp106/7 (centre) Owen Turville p107.